The Secret Life of a Black Aspie is a highly anticipated book worth waiting for! Prahlad takes the reader through his life journey, moving through generations and differing locations, challenging assumptions of the meanings, experiences, and feelings of blackness, disability, and gender. Prahlad's text is a thought-provoking mix of memories, images, and imaginations, with a strong dose of emotion. This is a terrific book!

—Michael Gill, Disability Studies Program, Syracuse University

This is a remarkable, important, brilliantly written book. For decades, people of color on the autism spectrum were overlooked by the medical establishment. In telling his own story with candor and grace, Prahlad not only delivers one of the most detailed accounts of being autistic to date, he relates the epic journey of a generation from the years following the end of slavery through the social upheavals of the late 20th Century. The passages of the book describing Prahlad's synaesthetic experience of the world are so vivid and intense they will haunt your dreams.

—Steve Silberman, author of *NeuroTribes: The Legacy of Autism and the Future of Neurodiversity*

Anand Prahlad recounts a life story that has never been told before. He takes the reader on a compelling journey from rural Virginia, to the San Francisco bay area's counter culture to a Midwestern college town. It is also an inward journey charting a consciousness with a compelling combination of dreamy lyricism and unflinching precision. *The Secret Life of a Black Aspie* fills a gap in the growing cannon of disability memoir, broadening our understanding of race, gender and neurodiversity. It is hard to put down and impossible to forget.

—Georgina Kleege, UC Berkeley
Author of *Sight Unseen* and *Blind Rage: Letters to Helen Keller*

The Secret Life of a Black Aspie

A Memoir

ANAND PRAHLAD

Text © 2017 University of Alaska Press

Published by
University of Alaska Press
P.O. Box 756240
Fairbanks, AK 99775-6240

Cover design and interior layout by Jen Gunderson, fiveninetydesign.com.

Cover art adapted from *Wanderlust Wonderland*, Collage on canvas, 2008,
by Krista Franklin, www.kristafranklin.com.

Library of Congress Cataloging in Publication Data

Names: Prahlad, Anand, author.
Title: The secret life of a black Aspie : a memoir / Anand Prahlad.
Description: Fairbanks, AK : University of , 2017. | Includes bibliographical
references and index.
Identifiers: LCCN 2016025136 (print) | LCCN 2016038645 (ebook) | ISBN
9781602233218 (pbk. : alk. paper) | ISBN 9781602233225 ()
Subjects: LCSH: Prahlad, Anand,Mental
health. | Asperger's
syndromePatientsBiography.
| Asperger's syndromePatientsFamily
relationships. | Husband and wifeBiography.
Classification: LCC RC553.A88 P73 2017 (print) | LCC RC553.A88 (ebook) | DDC
616.85/88320092 [B] dc23
LC record available at https://lccn.loc.gov/2016025136

"Without positive obsession, there is nothing at all."

Octavia Butler, Parable of the Talents

For Ruby, Jeremiah, Lizzy, and Beulah. For my children and my children's children.

And for my wife, Karen, without whom this book could not have been written.

A special thanks to the University of Missouri Research Board for a fellowship that gave me time to work on the book. Grateful acknowledgment to the journals, Fifth Wednesday, Water~Stone Review, *and* The Journal of American Folklore, *which published earlier versions of "Growing up with the Spirits," and "Born with the Spirits."*

Introduction: Remembering

Don't judge a book by its cover.

I first suspected that I might have autism spectrum disorder (ASD) when I read about autism as a university student. I was nineteen. I didn't get an official diagnosis, though, until I was fifty-seven. After decades in denial, I sought a diagnosis because I was finally willing to deal with it, because dealing with it seemed to be the only chance to save my relationship with my partner, Karen, now my wife. We sat in a quiet office as the therapist went over my test results and what they meant. I had high functioning ASD. Her voice was soft and soothing. She got me to the core, like no one ever had, and for a minute I was so happy I started crying. The feeling of being understood was so redeeming. But a second later, I was terrified. I started falling and landed at the bottom of a well. My tears turned the water in the well salty, and so I was thirsty but didn't have anything to drink. I folded inward, like a blossom that closes at night, and couldn't speak, and couldn't scream for help.

My whole life I had thought that I was from another planet, that someday the ship would come for me and take me home. I believed that most other people were insane and that I was one of the rare sane ones. Who else but crazy people would make a world that moved too fast to keep up? What sane people would make a world that left so little room for quiet, for thinking, for kindness, beauty, or grace? In what sane world would there have been slavery?

The feeling that I was from another planet gave life meaning. There was a reason for my suffering. There was a reason why I never really fit in. For why I so seldom had any feelings for many of the things people usually have feelings about. There was a reason why I couldn't remember things. Why everything around me seemed to be a noisy blur, moving too fast to catch hold of. Eyes and ears on my planet were different. They were suited to slower speeds. To lower pitches. I would be here on earth for a while and then I would go home. It would always be today the entire time I lived here, but that would change when I got home. I would remember yesterday then, and I would imagine tomorrow.

As part of my therapy, I started reading about autism. But the diagnosis and the books took away the two main things that helped me to function. They took away the hope that the ship would be coming, and they took away the pride I felt for being one of the few sane ones. Some of the things I read made me feel even more like a creature than I already did. Some of the words were so cold and clinical. The books described creatures that looked human but were something else. They often had limited capacity for empathy. It was questionable whether they were capable of love. They had problems with time perception. They were hypersensitive and prone to melt-downs, usually caused by overstimulation. They were often disasso-ciated from the social world. They needed routine; disruptions could cause severe problems with their functioning. They processed slowly and were sometimes mistaken for mentally defective. I didn't want those things to be true about me, but a lot of them were. And the books didn't talk about our gifts, the special things we can do that others usually can't. They didn't talk about the special light we bring.

Always feeling disconnected is one of the hardest things about my Asperger's. It's like when a white man who has never known a black person puts his arm around a black coworker and says some-thing like, "Hey, buddy, you gonna come and hang out with the guys tonight? We're going to knock down a few and watch the game." He's trying to be friendly. He wants to feel like they're the same. But they're not. Most things people say to me feel like that. People talk to me and they assume I'm hearing and understanding their words. But usually I'm listening to their colors. I'm seeing them. I'm feeling their temperatures. I'm smelling their scents. And whatever I see or smell or touch, I taste. Even if I don't want to. I have what they call "sensory integration dysfunction," or synesthesia. My senses are all mixed together. So, when I'm talking to people, I'm tasting them on my tongue. I learned to tell by my senses what people want, but that's different from knowing what they mean. Sometimes I desperately want to feel connected, but I just don't. Other times, I don't even notice that I'm not connected. I'm in my own bubble, and other people are in theirs.

We're using the same words, but we're speaking different languages. If people were talking about movies, for example, and I said I didn't like scary movies, someone would try to convince me that scary movies weren't so bad. They would think that we were talking about the same thing, a little thing, relatively speaking. But not many things are little to me, and if they were, I wouldn't bother talking about them. I don't know how to chitchat for more than three sentences, or around forty words. I don't get the point of it.

If I said I couldn't watch scary movies, I would mean I couldn't watch them because a girl would step out of them with blood on her dress. And unless I buried the dress in a certain kind of spot, I wouldn't be able to sleep on the right pillow. And if I didn't sleep on the right pillow, I would have the wrong person's dreams. And if I had the wrong person's dreams, I would wake up as the wrong person and do the wrong things, and it would take a long time to get the right person back. The right person would be wandering in purgatory for who knows how long while their life was falling apart. But the scary movie is only an example. It's like that with most conversations. What I mean is a domino in a long row of other dominoes that no one else can see or imagine.

It seems like most people's minds are telling them things to connect with other people's minds. But my mind is telling me things that make it hard to connect. My mind is telling me things that take me away from other people's worlds. Like if somebody is looking serious and they say something like "That was really sad what happened to that person" or "I think this requires serious consideration," do you know what my mind would tell me? It would tell me, "I wish I had some cherry jelly, like the kind in the little containers in restaurants. The kind you peel the top paper off. And the underside is silver. And you put it on your biscuits." It would tell me that because something in the person's voice was the color of cherry and I could taste it, but the taste was incomplete. "I wish I had some cherry jelly on a buttery bite of corn bread. That would be so good."

When it dawned on me in college that I might be on the spectrum, I decided that I wanted to work with autistic children. The urge to help out has always been in my bones. Maybe it's my way of paying the fare for being allowed to live. For not being locked in the basement or the closet. But when I tried working with kids on the spectrum, I quickly recognized I was too unstable. I fell apart too easily and spent most of my energy just trying to hold myself together. I couldn't be around severely autistic kids. Their screaming tore away the thin veils surrounding me, the veils that allow me to keep my form, to avoid turning into vapor. Being around others on the spectrum left me feeling naked and helpless, as frightened as if the world had fallen apart. When I stood in a room of six children on the spectrum, I fell into their worlds, like falling endlessly in a dream. All of the sanctuary in how things stay fixed in the neurologically typical world vanished. I floated like a fleck of yellow in a deep blue sea. I wanted to run, to find my way back to safety.

After that brief spell in college, I tried to forget about autism, and I tried not to let anyone else know. I tried not to let myself know. I never mentioned my suspicion to anyone, and tried hard when I was around people not to show any of the signs. The majority of people are not very nice to the disabled. They often dismiss us and imagine we don't exist. They build the world in ways that don't consider our existence. So fast! So sense-singular. I guess they feel like we're the weaknesses of the species, the worthless. The embarrassments. The signs of imperfection. The nightmares of their so-called beauty.

The old people I grew up around used to tell me stories about the plantation. Some of the stories about slaves make me think about people with disabilities. When the slaves were freed, the slave owners gathered them and said, "Y'all niggers is 'free' now. You are on your own now. You'll have to root, hog, or die." It's similar for people with disabilities. We have to root, hog, or die. Many people seem so agitated that some of us can't see what they see, or hear what they hear, or do things the way they do them. I've watched. They sometimes whisper and chuckle, even to me, not knowing who I am. Or they scowl or grimace, or their faces distort with pity. It was much worse when I was growing up, and when I was living most of my life, than it is now. That's why I've spent my life hiding my disorder, even being in denial. I have too much pride.

But now I want to talk about it. I want to tell you what it's been like, growing up black, in the South, with ASD, and trying to make it in life. As I've gotten older, I've started to function less effectively. I've become more like I was as a child. My personas and my filters have started breaking down. When I'm sitting in a restaurant, for instance, I can't stop hearing all of the conversations around me, or the patterns of silverware striking glasses and plates. The rhythm of the fans, cool or warm air blowing from ceiling or floor grates. It's that way everywhere. And so I hear only bits and pieces of what the people I'm sitting with are saying. Mainly, I watch their faces and their postures, and listen to the stories their bodies are telling, and add details to them with my imagination.

I'll try to describe having Asperger's and being black to you, as best I can, by telling you stories about my life. Being black and coming from the South are no small things. Nor is being older. Most people think of children when they think of autism. They think of people who can barely function enough to feed themselves or put on their clothes. They think of white, middle-class parents in suburbs or cities who can help their children. Most people have those pictures of autism because those are the ones on television, in magazines, and other places where there are books and articles. The pictures help to educate people. They tell them how to have the right amounts of sympathy and interest. They sensitize people. They tell them how to care about people on the spectrum and how to care about the words "autism" or "Asperger's syndrome."

The biggest thing about being an older black man with Asperger's is that the three things don't go together in most people's minds.

People don't have any pictures for it. It's like a woman with a beard or a man with breasts. Most of the pictures people have tell them that a black man equals toughness. Coolness. Anger. Stupidity. Ridiculousness. Brutishness. Pictures tell people that we don't have feelings, or that if we have them, they aren't as developed or as sensitive as those of white people. If you poke us with a sharp object, we won't feel it until it breaks the skin. And not much even then. Our bodies just don't fit with nice things. With sophistication or goodness. They fit with dirt. They fit with dark streets and soulless deaths.

No book or television show or movie has had characters like me. So people can't imagine me. They don't think that I exist. Even many of my friends. Therapists. People on the street. They don't know what to feel or in what amounts to have each feeling. Even black people have this problem. When I've told black people that I have autism, or Asperger's syndrome, they've often said, "No you don't." Or "Nigger, ain't nothing wrong with you." Or "All that shit is just in your mind." Or "You just lazy, that's all."

They think that what you see is what you get. That because I can hold a job, and do things that other people can do, I must be "normal." I couldn't have autism, first, because I'm not a child; second, because I'm black; and third, because I'm successful and can hold a job.

A part of the reason I've been able to hide my autism so well is because other people can't, or haven't wanted to, see it. It's an invisible disability. People don't like imagining difference, and so, when they can, they see what they want to see. So being a black man is like an accidental sleight of hand. Many white people simply can't see black people at all, much less see with the discernment it would take to notice Asperger's. And many black people can't believe in disabilities. They can't believe in anything that would make our "race" seem vulnerable. They want us to be like warriors or conquering heroes. And for most of my life, Americans had no general awareness of neurological disorders. The words, ideas, or pictures for ASD just didn't exist.

Being black with autism, and especially growing up when I did, has meant double troubles. It's meant that often I don't know where one thing ends and the other thing begins. If I was among a group of white people and didn't understand what was being said, was it because of Asperger's or because of race? Usually it was both. Then, add on the fact that I grew up on a plantation, in a family where almost everyone had neurological disorders. In some ways, though, this combination has helped to save me. Although I was more eccentric than anyone else in my family, I was still familiar. I still made sense to them. They could understand some of my dysfunctions, because they had them to a lesser degree themselves. They very patiently taught me many simple things about how to get along. How to create a habit and live by it. How to deflect sounds. How to guess what people wanted. Some of those things were what had helped slaves to survive. How to make a mask. How to scream silently.

Before I start telling you about my life, though, I should share with you a secret: I don't remember most of it. I don't remember most experiences I've had or most of the people I've met. I don't remember conversations I've had or the names of places I've been. I always feel like I just got here today. I always feel like I'm walking in a snowstorm and my tracks are being quickly covered over. My memory doesn't stick to things. It sticks to colors, and temperatures, and tastes. I remember mostly sensory details and ideas, because those are the things I experience as most real.

I've read that people with autism think in pictures, but I don't usually. I think more in feelings and senses. In colors and sounds. Even if I do sometimes see pictures in my mind, they never fit the words that people have for them. Not remembering things might have something to do with not seeing images in my mind. If you said, "Imagine a cat," I would imagine the way cats make me feel. But I wouldn't get a picture of a cat. If you said, "Imagine a lake," I would imagine the way the wind felt blowing across the lake. How the wind tasted. But I wouldn't get a picture. So, if we took a trip and stayed by a lake, I might remember the wind but not any of the other things that happened. And if you said, "Do you remember when we stayed by the lake?" I probably wouldn't.

Even when I do remember things, it's not when I'm trying to. My memories come as random feelings, whenever they decide.

Sometimes they're from some other life before this one. They have no time line; they just jump around. I try organizing them based on colors and tastes. It's sort of like organizing books in a library based on the way they smell. Except most of the books are not usually on the shelves. A book appears suddenly, and just as suddenly it disappears. An invisible library is what it is. I remember being in the kitchen with Mama while she was cooking. I remember going on a train. I remember getting a beating. I remember having a dog. But I don't have any clear pictures. The memories come like a breeze, a color, a feeling, and for a few minutes everything is heightened, like television in super HD. I close my eyes and tingle all over. I feel something like the density of colors. But it doesn't feel like a memory because it's always in the same moment I'm in. It's like a backward déjà vu. Memories are flavors. I close my eyes and stick my tongue out. No one calls this an orgasm, but sometimes it feels like one.

When I wake up in the morning, I don't remember yesterday. Most of the time I'm excited and happy. Everything is so new and astonishing. The sun is still the sun. It hasn't changed to something else. There are still clouds and the blue sky. There are still such things as closeness and distance. I still have all of my fingers. I can still see myself in the mirror. But I have to remind myself who I am and what I'm supposed to be doing. My mama said once, in concern, "If you ever got Alzheimer's, no one would know the difference." People imagine that you have to remember a lot of things to function, but you don't. You have to remember what's familiar. You have to remember ideas and rules.

I'm telling you my stories because I have to, for the same reason I have to organize my dishes and my food in the cabinets and the refrigerator. I have to organize the few things I remember. Maybe I won't forget them if I hear them being told. I'm telling you because I want to put my mind on display, like a painting on a wall. I want to share it the way you share things by talking to each other. This is the only way I know of doing that. The sharing is more the point than the stories. The way that I remember is more the point than the memories. The senses of things are more the subjects than the things. And maybe it will help someone else to hear the stories, someone with autism or someone with a loved one on the spectrum.

But before I begin, you have to agree to three things. First, you can't interrupt me while I'm talking. If you do, I'll forget what I was going to say, and it could take me months, or even years, to remember and start talking again. This is another way that ASD affects me. The part of my mind that concentrates is easily disrupted. So you can't ask me questions or start tapping on the table.

Second, you can't start looking in my eyes. Most people on the spectrum don't like for other people to look into their eyes, and I'm no different. They aren't your eyes; they're mine. They don't belong to you, and your gaze hurts. My eyes aren't public property. You have to ask first. When people start searching in my eyes, I want to run, or scream at them, or mess with them, or hurt them to make them stop.

The third thing to remember is that most of what I tell you is literal to me, even if it seems like I'm speaking in metaphors. People have been trying to take my experiences away from me all of my life by saying things like "You're so dramatic," "You exaggerate so much," "You're so extreme," or "It's all in your mind," as if their experiences aren't also in their minds. My mind works differently; that's all. If you put your hand on a hot stove, your brain would send a signal to your hand to make it jerk back off of the stove. If I walk into a room that's too bright, my brain would send the same message to my whole body. My descriptions are of what I really experience, not what I imagine. If I say my skin is on fire, I really mean it. If you can bring yourself to hear me literally, to touch my fire the way you touch a book, or water, or an apple, you'll understand the world I live in so much better. You'll understand why my real life is such a secret.

Born with the Spirits

Seeing is believing.

The mind is flame.
The body is a charm.
And neither one of them
is yours.

On the day I was born, my mama and daddy were living in a trailer in a small green meadow beneath a tree behind my great-grand-mother's, my granny's, house. They named me Dennis, after Dennis the Menace, anticipating that I would be a trickster. It was spring, and the yard was full of jonquils, wild onions, sparrows, and robins, with Leghorns and Rhode Island Reds, blue jays in magnolia and thrushes in the thickets. There was a hummingbird in the early crocus and a flock of canaries passing through like a wind too far in from the coast. It was March 12, 1954, in Virginia, the "Gateway to the South," when I was born, this time in a black body, on the out-skirts of Wickham Plantation.

Around the time that I was born, hippies hadn't been thought of yet. Chuck Berry was crossing over, riding on a red guitar like a black conked trickster. The *Brown v. Board of Education* case had ruled school segregation unconstitutional. Buckminster Fuller had just gotten the patent on geodesic domes. Martin Luther King, with all that he stood for, was already on fire. Rosa Parks was just about to board the bus. The smoke of Vietnamese jungles had already reached the shores of North America. Disneyland was having a grand opening. Linus was spotted for the first time with his beloved blanket. But no one would have known any of that where I was born, and if they had, it wouldn't have meant anything.

I was born on Canaan's Hill in a trailer beneath trees with pea pods and leaves that rustled the wind like feathers, beneath a totem tree—a tree touched by all of our ancestors. I don't know if Mama and Daddy were smiling the day I was born. We didn't have cameras yet, so there are no photographs. Our memories were left to our remembering, and I could never remember anything. So most of my childhood is just gone.

I don't know if Daddy was there in the room, or walking somewhere outside, happy, or pondering the burden of more children. I know they were worried, because the second child, born right before me, had died shortly after birth. They'd named him Baby Folly and buried him in a little white casket at the edge of the woods. When we were growing up, they never talked about it.

When I was home in 2011 for my summer visit, Mama showed me the spot where he was buried. She had hired someone to clear away the bramble and thickets so we could see it. None of us—me or my siblings—had ever seen the grave. He was just a blank space that haunted us like a ghost. My mama wanted me to be there when she cried for our brother. We stood for a while, just looking, saying nothing. Still, the words have an awkwardness to them coming out of my mouth. "Our brother."

Back when I was born they were nervous that I would also die. There was no doctor to deliver me, or any of us, out in the country. The white doctor sat in an easy chair in Ashland, the nearby town, maybe sipping from a cup of whiskey-tinged coffee. Maybe he was sleeping deeply and dreaming of nurses tenderly stroking his face. Maybe he had insomnia and couldn't sleep. Or maybe he was sleeping but not dreaming at all. The midwife eased me out. Our navels are marked by the way slaves cut and tied the umbilical cords, which was how our midwife still did it. She eased out two generations of us, birthed into her hands, in houses and shacks deep in the woods.

No one bothered much about the minute or the hour I was born. The details of births were not that important for people in those times. Someone ventured out of our jungle and into Ashland, weeks or months later, and scribbled on some papers the rough details of my birth.

I was born a Pisces, and all the things they say about Pisces would bear out, twice and three times over. Pisces is the sign of the mystic. We are old souls. We belong to some other magical, elusive reality. For us, ordinary life has little meaning. In fact, I never knew what ordinary life was.

The first things I remember seeing when I was able to see were the blossoms of a redbud outside the trailer window. I was stunned by their bright pink, pulpy stillness. I thought I was one of them. I thought that my body hung somehow in sea blue, a cluster of soft petals, suspended and still, floating in space.

The second thing I remember seeing was a slave spirit named Jeremiah. Jeremiah was a child it seemed, around eleven years old. He was standing beside the bed. When I looked away from his glowing, I could see his body in my head. He was brown and had bruises on his calves, a smile that warmed my soul, and a sadness that whistled through his bones. So then I thought I was like Jeremiah, a glow holding a body inside it like a book holding a story. Nothing touching nothing. Something plus itself.

The third thing I remember seeing when I was able to see was the brightness of my mama's face. I closed my eyes and the brightness still shone through, eclipsing all mirrors. It was so familiar. I would never grow tired of studying it. Its contours. Its many seasons. And then I thought my mama's body was my body, and her face was my face. A maple-brown expanse of garden glowing, with lips that moved on her whispers and breath like a butterfly's wings when it sits on a blossom.

Everything was still and quiet when I was born. There were no televisions. There were no sounds of radios. We had electricity, but only the most basic plumbing. There was a well in the yard with a crank wheel and a tin bucket that lowered slowly down the darkened well tunnel as you turned the crank, settled into the water, and ascended slowly when you turned the wheel in the other direction. When it squeaked I felt like dancing. Sometimes I did in my mind or with just my fingers. There was a pump house beside the well with a pump that moved water through pipes that Daddy buried in a trench leading to the house. The pump house was about three feet tall, eight feet square, and made out of cinderblocks. It covered a dug-out space, about the same dimensions, that housed the electric pump.

Water came trickling through the kitchen faucet. I could hear the water. I could feel it flushing through copper. I could hear it sit and wait, for hours, for days, like water in a lake, until we turned the handle on the faucet. And then it laughed like a trickster. Sometimes the pipes seemed angry, though, and they screamed at the water, roared as it rushed through them. I wondered about the water, what it felt like climbing up from so deep below the ground. I wondered if the water was where I came from.

Eventually, we had a bathroom, with a sink and faucets, but no toilet. We still had an outhouse and white porcelain buckets under our beds to pee in at night. Our pee sang in them at all hours. Our outhouses were always two-seaters, with dirt daubers buzzing in the ceiling corners near spider webs. White, powdery lime was sprinkled over the floor and periodically sifted down through the seats to cover the dark, soft mass of excrement six to eight feet below. We always ran a stick around the smoothed-down plywood underside of the seat hole, for spiders. The fear of black widows biting us when we sat down was as intense as the fear of any bogeyman.

The outhouse was like a little throne. A little cathedral. A little temple. A little meditation room. There was no time in the cathedral. I could sit and hear the web of bird voices take my body into a thousand directions and turn me into a listening pulse. A tingling. I could hear an airplane, hundreds of miles away. I could hear all the words my mama and granny and daddy and sisters and brothers and cousins blew out of their mouths, holding me. The screams of some girls. An axe splitting wood. Bees exploding with insistence. I could see the blue of the sky through cracks in the warped boards. Clouds. At night, I could disappear into the darkness, into the shower of stars, and I could feel them touching me with chilly hot fingers.

People had just started to get cars when I was a boy. One man still drove into town with his horse and buggy. I remember one day Granny saying that he had been hit by a car. The buggy had been flipped upside down, and he had been thrown into the grass-filled ditch that ran along Route 54. Granny and Mama were serious for a minute but then laughed, recalling stories about the man. They

often laughed at others' misfortunes, with little sentiment, especially if the things that happened resulted from stupidity. They couldn't
abide stupidity and had little sympathy for people who had difficul-
ties because they didn't use common sense or because they fooled
themselves into believing things they knew deep down weren't true.
I think that this was the way the slaves looked at people.

In the soil around our houses were the broken bodies of great-great-
great-great, great-great-great, great-great, and great relatives. Were
the bones and ashes of my family who had been slaves. Small fires
smoldered on green mounds in the yard, at the edges of the woods,
in clearings, among the fruit trees in the orchard and the young green
rows of corn, and in the many yards of houses hidden back through
the woods. Lost spirits walked back and forth, floating among the
leaves of maples and dogwoods and oaks. Some of them were lost,
and others were just watching over things. I could see them pass
through the sunlight. Under elms. Under the clothes hanging on the
line. Under the tall trees with leaves that were always in glory. Every
path we walked on was worn smooth, like the carved wood of a
walking cane. All the trees were also rubbed slick in places, first by
slaves, when they touched against them, rounding curves in the paths,
and then by the later generations.

   In the air were echoes of their calls and cries. There was a for-
lornness, a shadow we breathed. A numbness. Always something in
the air like the leftover smoke of a house fire. Like charred wood.
Like warm cinders. Like the leftover smoke of a lynching. The lin-
gering scent the next day, the next week, the next month, the next
year, and the next. Something like burnt nothing else. Not wood. Not
grass. Not old rubber, or clothing, or tar, or plastic. Something bitter
mixed with the sweet scents of honeysuckle, forsythia, and moist earth.

   It takes so much longer than anyone wants to admit to get over
being a slave, to get over being the grandchildren of people who
were in bondage. Because everything still remembers. The earth
remembers things. DNA remembers. Objects and things remember.

So we walked in a not belonging. A not being known by anything else other than the plantation. There was a sea of time without waves. But the waves would slowly ripple in, as the outside world did. Going to school was a ripple. Television and radio were ripples. Daddy going off to work as far away as Richmond was a ripple. But meanwhile, the old folks washed clothes, canned fruits and vegetables, walked with walking sticks, spat tobacco, laughed and cried, raised gardens, raised hogs and cows and chickens. Meanwhile, all of this was water whose surface never undulated, never broke, until later, when I was older.

People walked in shell shock. The shell shock we walked in would grow inside us and deepen, like oak and maple and sweet gum, elm, locust, and crepe myrtle seeds until one day we would be a forest of trees, trapped between time and no time. Aging and having children. And having the grandchildren. And the great-grandchildren. And the great-great-grandchildren. And the cousins. And the aunts. And the uncles. And the nieces. And the nephews. And the shell shock would keep washing over us like waves as we struggled to manage the modern world. It would wash over us like the sea over seashells, while outside the world would move on, imagining we did not exist, pretending we never existed, shoving us as deeply into the corners of its closets as possible. Now and then someone would pick us up, like a seashell, and put us to their ear, and they would hear the waves of ironic laughter that helped us to survive.

My community was located on the outskirts of Wickham Plantation, in Hanover County, Virginia, right in the middle of the state. Perhaps you've heard of Hanover. It's famous for the deep-red, fat tomatoes that grow there in the summer. And of course you've heard of Virginia. It's famous for its salt-smoked ham. It's where the first British colonies were formed and the first African slaves touched American soil. In Virginia, the air is always ripe and foggy with history. Each year, our school classes would take field trips to places like Monticello, Ash Lawn, the Washington Monument, and Jamestown. In school we learned the speeches of Patrick Henry—"Give me liberty or give me death"—the preamble to the Constitution, the Declaration of Independence, and so on. Statues of the Confederacy litter the landscape of cities and towns like Petersburg and Norfolk and Richmond.

In Richmond, "the capital of the Confederacy," there's a long cobblestone street called Monument Avenue that is lined with statues of Confederates. In the park at Virginia Commonwealth University, where I would eventually enroll, there's a statue of Captain Wickham, the man who "owned" my great-great-great-great- and great-great-great-grandparents, along with those of everyone else in my community.

Wickham was a descendant of Robert "King" Carter, one of the richest slaveholders and landowners in the seventeenth and eighteenth centuries. His mother was Robert E. Lee's first cousin. In fact, Lee's mother was born on Shirley Plantation, of which Hickory Hill—Wickham's 3,200 acres—was only a small part. Wickham's family on both sides were among the "First Families of Virginia" going back to the first colony. They sat in all the seats of power. They were founders of settlements, like Yorktown. They sat in governor chairs. Lawyer desks. House of Delegates rockers. In drafting and signing rooms for the Declaration of Independence. To us, though, they were slave owners, one step above the lowest form of life, slave drivers.

I have heard some of the old folks say that the Wickhams didn't whip their slaves as badly as some of the owners and overseers on surrounding plantations did theirs. But I've heard others say they were just as mean, that it was always six on one hand and half a dozen on the other. I remember my granny telling stories about Wickham and the other white bosses chasing and molesting or raping the black women and girls. And how her mother stood up to them. And how my great-great-great-, great-great-, and great-grandmothers stood up to them and tricked them to avoid being raped. Sometimes they called out to one of the other slaves, as if they needed help with something, when the bosses grabbed them. Or they acted like they were "crazy," and made jokes about poisoning them. The bosses were afraid of "crazy" slave women.

When the Emancipation Proclamation was signed, the Wickhams kept most of the slaves on as domestics or field hands. They kept the kingdom we had built and gave us nothing. They were never sorry. They never believed they had done anything wrong. To us, that was the essence of whiteness. The freed slaves moved across the border of the plantation, out of bondage, to "Canaan's Hill," and bought small acres of land and settled. My great-great-great-granddaddy gave it that name. You've heard this story. Some fled North and some stayed on. As far as freedom went, they had the freedom to leave, penniless, broken, uneducated, and alone. Or to stay and keep working on the plantation.

I grew up watching the descendants of the slave owners pass by daily on the road that led out of the plantation, going to and from town. Sometimes they would wave at us. We'd wave back. *Hi, slave owners.* The road was hard dirt and bald in spots that glistened in the sun like foreheads. There were dips and potholes in spots. When it was dry, the dust from car tires followed cars like trains of smoke. The dust got on everything. The shrubs along the road. On our skin. On hard surfaces of wood and glass in the house. Down our throats. The road was like a tunnel below archways of tall trees. Fields of soybeans or corn ran along one side, most of the way from Route 54 to our house. Woods ran along the other side, and then a neighbor's house, woods, and fields.

I walked by run-down slave quarters. I heard stories all the time about slavery. It was just yesterday. My daddy's daddy worked in Wickham's dairy. My daddy's mama worked in the big house. She gathered eggs. Churned butter. Made biscuits. Cleaned floors. Did laundry. She cooked in a big iron skillet. My granny's mama worked in the big house. Her husband worked in the fields. I heard stories about my cousins and uncles and aunts and grandmothers and grandfathers and things that happened on the plantation. I saw their spirits all the time. Walking in the yard. Sitting under the elm tree. Sometimes I would go and sit with them, to feel their quietness. It was like falling into a soft blanket. Into the space where no one blinked, no one breathed.

When I was five, I would fall sometimes when I felt lashes sting my back. I'd be chasing a ball my brother threw or running in high grass, for a moment starting to feel happy, to believe in happiness. But suddenly a lash would cut me across my back. I would lie face-down in grass or dirt, in a yard I didn't recognize, screaming. Daddy or someone else would take me into the house and lay me in the bed. I felt safe in Daddy's arms at times like that. I could feel his love in the way his palm curved under me and almost levitated me. People sometimes carry love in their palms. Sometimes they carry anger. Mama and Granny would boil water in an old blackened iron kettle, pour it into a basin, and dip a washcloth in, wring it out, and gently wash over the welts that had mysteriously appeared on my back. Still, today, I am comforted by the sound of water dripping from a wash-cloth as someone wrings it out. I often stand at the sink, wringing.

Not long after I was born, my daddy built a house across the yard from Granny's, and we moved out of the trailer. Our house was a make-do affair, patched up as crises demanded. My daddy built it as best he could with the little bit of wood that he could accumulate. Some two-by-fours and a lot of plywood. His brother, Uncle Matt, helped some with the roof. Both of them were good carpenters, but they had limited resources. The house was added to when the seams were about to burst. The roof of our house often leaked, and the siding was torn. Nothing was finished or straight. We had fans in the sticky hot summers and an old wood stove in the cold winters. Ours was not so different than other little houses of poor people you would see if you drove through the rural South in the 1950s, or even now, in many places.

My family included my mama and daddy and six kids—my older brother Richard, (three years older than me), my younger brother Levi (two years younger than me), my sister Thelma (a year younger than me), and Jean (five years younger than me). In the beginning, the kids shared one room and two beds. Later on there was one room for the boys and another for the girls. The sixth child,

Angie, was born fourteen years after Jean. By then my daddy and my older brother were gone. Daddy had left shortly after Mama became pregnant with Angie. He was busy having other families, who he stayed with until the kids were preteens and then left them and started up again with another woman.

For all of its shortcomings, our house may as well have been a mansion. It sat near Providence Road, once known as Hickory Hill Road, atop Canaan's Hill, where a bloody Civil War battle was rumored to have occurred and where one of the many headless horsemen who haunted the countryside was supposed to still ride on full-moon nights, searching for his head. Our house was pulled in four directions. It was pulled up the road, which led to the town, commerce, "progress," impending integration, technology, and the rest of the world. It was pulled down the road, which led back to slavery and the heart of the plantation. And it was pulled across the road, in both directions, to cousins and more cousins, the souls of ancestors, to different sets of paternal and maternal longings. You might say we sat at the crossroads, waiting for the devil to come, struggling to know what we would do with our souls when the critical moment came.

Daddy used to tell us stories about the devil and the crossroads. Often on Saturday morning in the summertime he would take us bright and early into the woods to pick blackberries. It was earlier than the sun wanted to rise, when there was still dew covering the grass and leaves, and giant black-and-yellow-striped spiders sat in the center of large dew-beaded webs. We'd bring buckets of berries back, hands painted purple, and Mama would fry them up and put them over waffles, alongside salt fish or bacon or sausage from the smokehouse.

"If you want to learn how to play the guitar," Daddy would say when we'd walk by this particular juncture heading toward the Wickham big house, "just come to the crossroads at sunrise. The devil will meet you here. And he'll offer to buy your soul. If you sell it to him, he'll give you the gift, and you'll be able to make that guitar cry and sing. Now, sometimes he won't take no for an answer, and he'll follow you, promising you all sorts of things. Money, nice clothes, women. If that happens, they say, you should keep repeating, 'What in the name of the Lord God do you want?' They say evil can't stand to hear the name of the Lord. He'll have to leave you alone then."

But it wasn't just a story. It was a warning that everything comes with a price. It meant that those who had things (mainly white people) had traded in their souls. It meant the only road off the plantation was to bargain with the devil. As I was to learn later, the devil couldn't care less about how many times you call on the name of the Lord.

My granny's house sat farther back from the road and was not as fractured as my family's. It was an older two-story house, built in the days following the end of slavery, and it was the nicest house built on Canaan's Hill. Among other things, we were a family of artisans, and it was taken for granted that we would just know how to do basic things like carpentry. After all, we were the labor that built the "master's" houses and the other buildings on the plantation, that did most of the ironwork, the stonework and masonry, and the landscaping. We held generous visions of houses and yards.

Granny's house had a good-size living room with a sofa, chairs, tables, and corner stands with glass ornaments. It had a large bedroom downstairs, also with vintage furniture. It had a big kitchen and a formal dining room with a well preserved, oak China press, and an oak table and chairs with barley-twist-style legs. It had tongue-and-groove wood floors. It had a bathroom, but without running water, and two bedrooms upstairs. Our granddaddy's musket sat in a corner of the dining room, and a sheathed military sword sat in another. One of my favorite places in Granny's house was the large pantry under the stairs. Stocked with jars of canned foods, it was always cool and smelled like pinewood and peaches, and white potatoes, onions, furniture oil, and canned grape jelly and plums.

The jars of jam sang and talked to me. They mesmerized me with the colors of their light. I spent hours with the pantry door closed, listening to them, watching them, being soothed. One of my favorite things to do was to watch flecks of dust floating in streaks of light or sunshine. They seemed so magical and so hypnotic. Sometimes I would close my eyelashes just a little and make everything rainbows. In the pantry, light came through the cracks in the door. The door was made of vertical rows of boards, painted light yellow on the outside, like washed-out mustard, like saffron or daffodils mixed with cream.

With the light on, I could lose myself for hours to the flecks of dust or rainbows on my eyelashes. Or I could reach up and tug on the string that turned the light off, curl up on the floor, and lose myself in just listening. To the floor creak. To water laughing in a pipe. To the jars singing.

A large arbor encased in wisteria vines the size of anacondas hovered over the pathway leading to the front porch, which ran the length of Granny's house. There were benches built in on either side beneath the arbor, and sometimes we sat or played there. The wisteria sprouted long, fuzzy green pods that were fascinating to touch and play with. Sometimes spirits could also be seen playing there. Mainly though they gathered in Granny's house.

In Granny's house I learned the footsteps of spirits, their pulses, their heat. How they come and go between dimensions. How to be possessed by them. How to feel their joy and sorrow. How they travel through light. I learned by watching them walk to and fro in dispossessed dimensions.

As children, we were frightened by the footsteps, hot spots, and occasional objects moving without visible explanation. At first I ran in fear. The sound of dimensions colliding, one erupting into another, was terrifying. Sometimes there was an awful smell when spirits came, although it was often sweet. It smelled like the earth at the roots of morning glory. But it was mixed with something like the sickening pollen that sumac spewed, or the nauseating, dense steam of boiled roots of sassafras. As I grew older, I grew more accustomed to the spirits, less afraid. I spent a lot of time in Granny's house, which was a gateway between centuries, a vortex for moving back and forth between worlds. It was not quite in the nineteenth century but not quite in the twentieth either.

Besides the spirits, there were also the unexplainable lights. We saw them with our other eyes, looking away. We felt them with the hairs on our skin. No one knew what to call them or what they were about. I remember hearing words like "guardians." Like "angels." I was drawn to the sudden doors out of which they came and through which they disappeared. I was struck by how the openings and closings of those doors changed time, stripped it of any weight. When the lights moved toward the portals, glowed brightly, and disappeared, I followed them. Sometimes I sensed them leaving, even if I wasn't in the room. I was led by aromas of burnt rosewood and the oil people used to tan leather with. I stood at the doorways, sometimes for hours, peering in. Sometimes, inserting a foot, a finger. Listening to a faint whirring sound. Feeling a wind on my skin as if I was standing at the end of a tunnel, a hallway. Listening to nothing.

One of the treats of childhood was spending the night at Granny's house. Granny was born on April 20, 1898. She was old when I was a child. But she wasn't old to me. Sometimes I thought of Granny as my best friend. Before we were born, she lived in her house with her husband (Walter, "Unc Wa Wa"), her sister (Marie, "Aun 'Ree"), her children (Grandma Arlene and Douglass), her grandchildren, and other people whose names I don't remember. But Douglass died as a young man from TB, Wa Wa died, Aun 'Ree married and moved into Ashland, Grandma Arlene left and went to New York to find better and to be in the city life, and only Mama was left. Then Mama got married and built a house across the yard.

So, well before we came, Granny had lived alone. She made her own meals, did her own laundry, cleaned, kept her own flowerbeds and vegetables, climbed ladders and picked fruit from trees, baked the rolls for church communion, and occasionally did ironing or other work for white people. I remember her "putting down" rolls on Saturday evenings. Kneading the sweet-smelling dough and molding perfect, rounded rolls on baking pans, her hands and fingers coated in dough and oil and sifted flour. She was transfixed as she worked. She would cover them with light dish towels overnight while they rose, like living things, and put them into the oven first thing Sunday morning.

I remember Granny humming as she made dinner. Boiled rice and chicken feet. Biscuits and gravy. The tin saucepan and the iron skillet she cooked in. The clicking of the knob on the old white porcelain gas stove. The slight hissing, and then the whoosh of blue flames. Sometimes I got lost in the blue flames. Just watching them, I would forget everything else. I was always forgetting everything else. Granny would squeeze my shoulder gently to bring me back. Or she would start talking to me until gradually I could refocus and hear her. Then she would go back to cooking and start singing an old spiritual or hymn. At the end of a line she would take a deep breath, inhale the words back into her mouth, and then exhale them for the next line. Granny's breath was my heartbeat.

I felt special those nights, apart from the busyness and brightness of my family's house.

I remember sometimes lying awake in bed while Granny hummed and did things in the kitchen. Sometimes I fell asleep before she came to bed. I remember sometimes in the night trying not to be afraid as invisible footsteps approached, stopped, and were silent for what seemed like long periods while Granny talked to them. But they never left with footsteps. They simply turned and vanished into the dark. Sometimes I heard the sounds of someone sitting in a chair or coming down the stairs. Sometimes I thought I smelled them, the strange scent of moldy and foreign times and places. The sweat of slavery. The burnt stench of gunpowder from the Civil War. Pig musk. Hickory.

Images of Granny's reactions remain, burned into me, like sodium burned into a photograph. Especially if it was Walter, the great-granddaddy we never knew. He once held my older brother, Richard, in his arms, but he was gone by the time I got here. I never touched him. He died of lung disease. We saw a sepia-colored photo of him, in an army uniform, and another photo of him and Granny when they were very young. He was tall and handsome, and everyone said he was very kind. When he came, Granny would whisper inaudibly, her eyes fixed on something that I could feel but could not see. Her face reminded me of times when a joy would erupt from her as she sat and hummed, rocking on the porch or in the living room, clapping her hands suddenly and vibrating with something like electricity. Granny would say "Gone on to sleep" when she realized that I had been watching, peering from beneath covers I had pulled over my head, entranced by the curve of the rocker, by the squeaking song it kept singing.

Growing Up with the Spirits

Can't live by bread alone.

Both my mama and granny "saw things," and I inherited their gift. The gift was handed down on my mother's side. In the DNA, I guess. It helped us survive in slavery. To know things. To know what we needed to know but were never told. It helped us learn to read, to read all things. To know when someone would be sold, when someone else would be coming. To know what people wanted before they started talking. Before they even got to our house. To know yesterday, when the thought first lighted on them, like a sparrow on a branch. To visit those far away and never leave home. Mama and Granny often shared their dreams, especially dreams about things to come. The evenings were filled with talk about such dreams.

"Lord, I dreamt about cousin so and so last night," Granny would say. "Looks like she was wearing a red dress and was walking in a wedding. I was trying to get in speech of her, but every time I got close, she was somewhere else. I caught up with her finally, and she had these terrible bags under her eyes. Lord, Jean, looked like they were black, just as black as soot. Like someone who hadn't been sleeping, or had been cryin'. And then she said, 'Clara, it's such a beautiful wedding, isn't it? Now, at last I can rest.'" I seldom knew the people they were talking about, but I listened closely. I listened for some intangible essence of those people whose faces I would probably never see.

Sometimes they would describe people and tell stories about them. "They're just coming to check on us," they would say, or "I think so and so was trying to bring us a message." Maybe they were just missing us. Maybe they were stranded on islands of loneliness. The stories I heard were filled with insights about human nature, with laughter and warmth. The sounds of Granny and Mama telling those stories opened invisible windows and doors, and winds blew through the windows from other dimensions, bringing strange, sweet, and musky scents and making my skin tingle. Bodies without bodies walked through the doors, touching things, stirring the air and the dust.

Sometimes after having dreams, Mama and Granny would plan a trip to visit the person in the dream, and they would take me along. I never really wanted to go and stand by the side of elderly people, being a part of their aging, illnesses, or dying. Their houses smelled funny, and I felt so out of place. I would have to be afloat because there was nothing I could touch. Old dark wood. Smelly linoleum that touched me through my shoes and spewed mold into my lungs and dampness in the space around my bones. Soiled curtains that tinted the little light that came through with phlegm. To help, I'd carry a favorite rock or a piece of bark in my pocket. The whole time I was away from home I would never let go of it. I'd be rubbing it and squeezing it, and I would be more with my bark than with the people. *Why me?* I would wonder. The rocks and bark would answer, moving in my fingers like little secret children.

The old people were always happy that I'd come. That made me feel special. But, the burden of it. Like Jesus. My parents wanted a child like Jesus.

Sometimes the people we visited would simply let me stand in Mama and Granny's shadows. Other times they wouldn't. "Lord, Lord, now which boy is this, Jean? It's so nice that you've come." Someone would answer, "Yes, Lord" or "Ummm huh, it sure is. To see a young person taking interest today." "Well, thank the Lord." Sometimes they would rub my head or cup my small hands in their wrinkled and firm ones and look into my eyes. There'd be a little small talk. Granny or Mama would ask, "How are you feeling?" and they would answer slowly, "Well, you know this old body ain't what it once was" or "Clara, I'm just hanging on by the grace of the Lord." Granny would stand with both of her hands holding her purse in front of her, her body still, and great expression in her face. Mama's feelings came out in her body, her hands touching different parts of herself: her hips, her chin, her cheek, the other hand. She'd touch the wooden end of the bed, the bedspread, a glass of water; she'd touch the words as they came out of her mouth.

During some of those visits, I saw weakened spirits beginning to detach themselves from bodies, and I saw struggles to hold on. I saw terror in people's faces. I saw pain in their bones and in the tunnels inside their marrow. I saw overwhelming longings. I heard the sounds of butterfly wings brushing against each other, the noise of ripping, like the tearing of cloth. Butterflies spread out in my mind like dark flocks of sparrows when light is slowly leaving dark-blue skies. I whispered to them, as their wings reached out to touch me— me, a child. As their fragile weights pressed against me to save them, to forgive them, to take and keep some private part of them, breathing. All I could ever do was whisper. I felt guilty that I couldn't do more. Couldn't save them. And I felt angry that I had been asked to. I wanted to go back home.

Once, Granny took me to Baltimore to Cousin Molly's funeral. I'm not even sure if she was really my cousin. People were called "Uncle" something, or "Aunt" something, or "Cousin" or "Grandpa" or "Grandma" or "Sis" or "Bro." But the children seldom knew what they were to us. Everybody called someone Cousin. But whose cousin were they, really?

Cousin Molly was one of the old people who took a special shine to me. Like Unc' Tommy. When she appeared from Baltimore, she used to hold me and make pretty sounds and smile and treat me like a little king. The birds sang when she held me. She smelled like perfume and potatoes. She whispered and breathed sweet blue seeds in my ear. I rested my head on her and sighed, and rested with the sunlight on maple leaves for what felt like forever, and then I let go. Mama hated when Cousin Molly left to go back to Baltimore, because I was so inconsolable. I thought that I was dying. My body convulsed. My head grew so heavy that my neck couldn't hold it up. Cousin Molly had spoiled me, they said. Being spoiled meant someone treated you so special that you started to expect it. After Cousin Molly left, if no one held me I cried so hard that someone would have to pick me up. But even in their arms I protested. I held my body straight as long as I could, looking at them, mooing like our cow and sucking slobber on my thumb.

When Cousin Molly died, I was about seven, and Granny took me on a train to Baltimore. At the funeral I rode in a long black car beside Granny and almost fell asleep. All the old people rubbed my head and pressed their hearts on me. They wore long wool coats and their hats were a sea of flower blossoms and feather-adorned saucers. Granny cried and closed her eyes and sang, "Couldn't hear nobody pray / couldn't hear nobody pray / down in the valley by myself / couldn't hear nobody pray." After the funeral we went to somebody's house and ate greens and corn bread and chicken. We rode home on the train carrying a big, warm Mason jar that held inside it the pieces of somebody's soul.

My sisters and brothers couldn't see the spirits, but I could see them. The spirits I loved the most were Jeremiah and Beulah and Lizzy. They were all slave children who often played with me. They looked like shadows, except they were closer to light, a different shade of light.

Beulah was a bittersweet, sassy presence who seldom talked. She had a sadness. She had a kindness in her heart that eclipsed her pain. She was always praying, even when she played. Sometimes I would look at her, sitting under the locust tree in summer heat or standing with me under the holly in winter, the silence of the snow deepening, widening, and for seconds she would almost disappear. And because she didn't always talk, I sometimes had to see her to know where she was, even when I could feel her. I liked to touch her arm and bump her shoulder with mine. I liked to keep her in my sight so I could see the dark glowing complexion of her skin. It wasn't really brown or really black. They don't have words for some of our colors yet, however beautiful we may be. If she stood behind me, I could feel her, but barely, like the end of a wind.

Lizzy was the orange of autumn leaves. The orange fire of maples. The orange light the leaves cast beneath cities of trees in the field, in the woods, at dusk, in the second orange of sunset. She was the smile of having gone beyond flesh and still holding, still being, still filled with heart. When she walked into the room, I couldn't help but smile. She was what I could never be—she never fell apart. She never seemed confused about who she was. She just went into the day with her arms open. It never seemed to occur to her to be afraid or worried. Her voice was like the water inside laughter. The *shhhhhh* that kept going after the laughter stopped. Her voice wrapped around my skin like cotton and made me feel safe.

Jeremiah looked like the light under a damson plum on the evening of a sunny hot day on the first of August. Purple swirled inside him like the pink does in clouds in the western sky when the sun is setting. He was the sweetness of the hour before the dawn in broad daylight, the heart of my heart, the song of my songs. Oh, I reveled in him. His blue-black like blackberries. When I woke up, I often looked into his eyes and smiled. I laughed just to see him. I would kick my legs in the air and dance on my back. Joy would break me apart at the seams.

Whenever I was sick, Jeremiah was always with me, in the corner of the room when others were present and right beside the bed when others were gone. He sang to me and told me stories. He often played jokes. When I wondered about things, I could always ask Jeremiah, and if he didn't know the answer he'd make one up. He'd start talking with an impish smile on his face, and then I'd know a story was coming. The spirits' talking wasn't like people's. It was quiet, like smoke.

I asked Jeremiah once who the wind was, and where it came from. How could it suddenly appear and disappear? Was the wind a woman or a man? How could it stay invisible? He said he didn't know—he wondered the same thing. "But the night is something you can walk on," he said. "Like a road." And if you followed it to the end, the invisible things would lose their cloaks. "Let's walk on the night," he said. And I would try it for a while, but always I would get frightened and turn back.

The darkness outside where I was born was so unbroken you could walk on it. You could swim in it. You could open your mouth and feel it pouring down your throat, filling up your belly. There were no artificial lights nearby. No canopy of effervescence like the ones that hover over cities. It was solid and pure and alive with the distant brightness of the moon and stars. It was one of the last spots like it, I suppose, on the slowly brightening planet.

I learned not to ask Jeremiah about some things, though, because they made him sad. One time when Mama and Daddy were not getting along, I asked him what I could do, if I was doing something wrong that caused them to be upset. "I don't know," he said. "I never had a mama and daddy the way you do. They was sold off. There was a woman who was like a mama, though. They called her Aunt Rachel. She looked out for me in the tobacco fields. The leaves would sometimes cut my arms and hands."

That night when we went to bed, Mama thought I was crying because of something she said. But I was thinking about Jeremiah. "And Lord bless Jeremiah," I added to my prayers. I cried myself to sleep.

My granny and my mama and my daddy taught me so many things. I learned them like I was one of the old people, struck with amnesia, slowly remembering. There were many lessons about the nature of plants and our connections to them, about how they feed us something more than vegetables and fruit, more than the nutrients the physical body drinks. I clung to Mama and Daddy in the gardens and orchard, in the barns and henhouses and fields. We always raised a garden, with staples of corn, string beans, butterbeans, peas, beets, white potatoes, sweet potatoes, tomatoes, squash, carrots, watermelons, lettuce, and greens. We also had fruit trees: plums, apples, peaches, and cherries, as well as strawberries, raspberries, grapes, and blackberry vines. Each summer, we'd can vegetables and make jams and jellies.

My parents and Granny were always talking to the plants. Touching them. Exchanging cells. Some summer evenings I would stay behind in the garden with them while my brothers and sisters ran off to play. They'd walk along the rows of corn stalks, beans and tomatoes, stopping occasionally. Mama in the snap peas. Daddy in the corn. Bats filled the sky, their rubbery wings flapping, dipping erratically for insects. The speckled light of lightning bugs slowly surrounded us. Whippoorwills called. Mama and Daddy stood quietly, hands on the leaves, eyes closed, turning green, still as stalks.

We also shared blood with animals. We had pigs, chickens, cows, a horse, ducks, dogs, and lots of cats, and I heard stories about the guinea hens, peacocks, and goats that were there before I was born. I especially loved the chickens. They were so pretty, and each one had its own personality. Personalities with feathers, wings, clawed feet, sharp yellow beaks, hisses, squawks, and clucks. They looked at you sideways, as if you were from another planet. They strutted and scratched and skittered across mounds of dirt, into the bosom of hedges and underbrush, knowing something we didn't—we needed them more than they needed us; they were here first, and they would be here when we were long gone.

Granny once told me it had always hurt her to kill chickens, even though our family chose what they considered the most humane way. "It just didn't seem right," she said. "I told my mama that once. I remember it like it was yesterday. She was working in Wickham's house and it was coming on Christmas. They always killed a lot of chickens and ducks around Christmas. And we always had to pluck 'em and clean 'em. I would hate to see the chickens and geese killed. They were always around the yard, and I guess if you're a child you get to know them. Then you have to put their heads on the block and chop it off. Mama said, 'I understand how you feel, Clara, but we have to kill 'em. It's just their time.'"

Our family held the chickens by the feet, stretched them out, head down on a wooden stump, and brought the hatchet down with one swift stroke across their necks. Then we'd pitch them into the yard to dance around headless, wings flapping, like firecrackers, until the life finally went out. My own body heaved, watching them, listening to the sounds of their weight thumping against the ground, their chests swelling and deflating long after their feathers came to rest. Something scary opened up and part of me came alive in the opening, and I could not stop watching. The top of the chopping stump, with its inlays of hatchet marks rubbed smooth with dark stains of blood, was a touchstone in the middle of the yard.

The hatchet we used was the same one Cousin Betty hid in her apron the day the big freedom bell rang. That day, Granny told me, the slaves were all out working in the field, and the big freedom bell rang. Grant had taken Richmond. They all threw their hoes and axes and pots down and started jumping up and shouting and crying. The sky got brighter. Screams rose from the plums, and shouts of joy rose from the corn and tobacco and wheat sheaves and apples. A dam burst, and red clay bled. Some of them just stood in the field and in the yard, crying like babies. So glad, so glad to be free, so glad to be free.

While this was happening, Cousin Betty had taken the hatchet and set out for the big house, going to cut up ol masser. Uncle Prophet caught up with her, though, and pleaded with her not to do it. She finally handed him the hatchet, and he held her in that field until the burden of her tears flooded the creek, and it rose, and the screams from the scars on her back subsided. He held her until the mules brayed and the spirits beneath the wheat got up and walked. He held her until she broke down and cried just like a baby. Then he lifted her up and carried her back to the quarters and laid her in the bed.

We also butchered hogs and sometimes cows. The whole community came. It was one of my favorite but dreaded times. There were so many people, many of whom we seldom saw. Boundaries marked by rivalries or airs that dictated our usual day-to-day social life seemed to dissipate. People came together as they had since slavery when there was work to be done. These were the last days when we would celebrate a collective survival, before the embarrassments of things that had happened to us years ago, things we had done or had not done would stand up like walls between us. Before the will of the outside world pried us further apart.

Early that morning, the pigs would see the shadows of their deaths dancing and begin squealing and banging against the boards of the pen. The men would spill into our yard, and then the women. They would string rope around a pig's feet and hoist it upside down on a scaffold. With one smooth stroke, someone slashed the pig's throat, and a fountain of bright red gushed out. And then the air was red. The trees were red. The water in Mama's glass was red. The men stood in reddened light, joking and laughing as they waited for the blood to drain, for the light inside the pig's body to go out. The pig's eyes lighted on me as he spun slowly, wiggling. At first I cringed with the brightness of his terror. And then I laughed and couldn't stop laughing.

When the life had finally fled, the men built a fire, lowered the pig and singed the hair off, scraping and then cutting, and all the while so serious and austere but bantering, musical with their voices and their bodies. "Yeah, Richard, that's it, that's it. Now, over this way, a little bit farther." "Oh man, don't you know it!" I could hear back rooms and crap games, jail cells and juke joints and clubs filled with scents of piss and whiskey and perfume and other women's scents. The women wore aprons and poured pans of scalding water into large porcelain tubs. Later, their fingers wove ground meat, fresh sage, pepper, and salt into sausages. Children ran and played while I stood watching, almost like stone. I broke through the red day now and then by sliding my right foot back and forth along the ground and laughing. When I dared look up, I could see the spirits of dead pigs, like red kites, hovering on the wind.

Everyone said that animals could see beyond our veils. Our cows, for example, spotted spirits. When we walked them back through the woods on paths or roads grown over with weeds, they'd often stop abruptly, staring at a spirit, refusing to go on. Those roads and paths passed by sites where old houses had once stood. The rubble of fallen brick chimneys was usually the only thing remaining. People had picked through the rubble long ago and taken whatever furniture, wood, glass, or iron might have been of value. Now and then we'd find an old tarnished or fire-blackened dish, bottle, or piece of broken metal. We'd hear the stories about the people who had lived there. Spirits often hovered near such sites, especially if they were around turns in the road where there were "caves" made by the curvatures of overhanging branches filled with still shadows and interplays of darkness and light.

In the space between shadow and light were doorways through which spirits came and went. A thin membrane between form and formless. Patches of light-green ground cover grew between random red bricks. Its leaves huddled close together, becoming one large, expansive organism teeming with a will, with audible breath. It called to me. "Stay in the woods. Stay with us. We'll show you things." I'd move closer to Mama then, holding on to her leg, peering into the thickets beyond the rubble, into dark spots where slave children looked out. They were in dingy white rags, their hair uncombed, their black, boney legs whitened ashy. I'd imagine the woods at night, filled with spirits and plants reaching out, and I would scream silently.

These caves were not just in woods far from home. They were all around us. Often I'd be playing in our woods or under trees in the yard and I would pass through them. I'd feel ripples of air as solid as spring waters. Or a chill like winter that made me vomit and lose my orientation. Soon afterward, I'd be in bed, delirious with another unexplained illness. I'd lie in drenched sheets as sweat poured from my feverish body. My mama and granny knew that there were plants that could draw the illness out, but they didn't know which ones. This knowledge had been lost with the deaths of the older people, leaving us stuck somewhere between a foreign world of white doctors and an absence tied to our ankles, filled with pain.

Sometimes in bed I left my body and looked down at it from far above. I floated. I flew. I pondered whether to return; at least, I imagined that I had a choice. But I did return, drawn back by the smells of Mama's cooking, the clatter of pans in the kitchen, her voice, my granny singing, the chatter of my sisters and brothers, my daddy's knee, the warmth of newly changed sheets on my skin. And because in the breezes that blew in the spring or summer window, spirits would caress my face and whisper, "You have to go back. Go back."

The Pillows Are Crying

Still waters run deep.

Between one and ten years old, I was known as a child who cried all the time, at the drop of a hat, and who had frequent episodes of uncontrollable rage. They called me "tender hearted," and no one ever knew how much or what they could say or do around me, or to me. My rage was that of a cornered and wounded animal. It frightened those around me. My mama and daddy would tell me when I was almost grown how afraid they had been that I might seriously hurt someone. I was like someone possessed, they said. Like an angry demon inside their angel. Like someone "not right in the head," not wholly human. And I felt like something different. Something wrong. Sometimes I would try walking with my head tipped to the side, my arm thrown over it, like I had seen parakeets do, when they sleep with their heads under their wings, to see if the world looked more right.

Most of the time, I felt overwhelmed. Overstimulated. Frustrated. Out of control. Things around me moved too fast. People said things and moved on as I waded through the multitude of sounds around me, trying to separate out their words. Until I was around eight years old, the outlines of shapes around me were fuzzy, and things often seemed to melt into each other. When I first rode on a roller coaster, as a young adult, I recognized the nauseous, sick feeling of speed and fear as what I had been feeling "normally" most of my childhood.

Almost everything made me sick. My own emotions made me physically sick. The emotions of others around me made me sick. The thoughts of others made me sick. I could hear their thoughts. I could see them floating through the house like crowds of puppets going back and forth across the stage, wearing countless faces, carrying countless weights. Like bodies on a crowded city street. My thoughts would be lost in the multitude, and I could seldom find them. I came apart like a sack of grain, everything spilling out. I would lie in bed, an empty body searching desperately to be filled.

Touching the wrong spirits made me sick. The cries of objects, like the pillows, hoes, pots, axes, knife blades, doorknobs, glasses, coins, buttons, tables, and lamps made me sick.

The knives were always crying, "Marry me to the bright blood blossoms of your palms, your wrists, your arms, the insides of your thighs." The high pitch of glasses crying almost made me scream.

The snoring of the plants when they thought no one could hear them often made me sick. Sometimes it healed me. But the way they shrieked when they heard footsteps approaching made me tiptoe. Sometimes it made me stand still and not move at all, just so they wouldn't be afraid.

The brightness of sunshine was the same way. The loud brightness of the sunshine. Some days, it struck me down like fire burns up a blade of dried grass. Other days it propped me up like the wood beneath a scarecrow.

The buttons cried fake tears to see if they could trick me into weeping for them or holding them or putting a coat or a dry washcloth or a pillow over them to keep them warm. They were always getting cold.

Sometimes someone stepped on a leaf and I burst into tears. Or someone moved a marble I had set on a ledge to keep the world balanced, to keep my heart from sinking. Finding it gone, I would feel like I was plummeting down an abandoned well. I would spend days at the bottom, cold and wet and sucking my thumb. I would spend weeks after that climbing out. Sometimes while I was climbing, someone would start talking to me. My daddy was famous for talking to me at the wrong time. "How's my little man?" he would say, or "Come here, Red. Sit with your daddy." Or he would try to play running around or something like that. Or my brothers would jostle me or pull the covers off at night when I was almost to the top of the well. And as soon as I paid attention to them I would forget to hold on. I would lose my grip on the sides of the well and fall back to the bottom. Mama and Granny usually left me alone when I was climbing out. They would hum or sing to help me stay focused.

Some days someone would let the screen door slam, and I would imagine Daddy's gun had gone off, that Mama had shot him and he lay bleeding on the kitchen floor, while white chickens pecked in the yard. I would think her anger had burst, and he lay torn up inside, like when a bullet entered the belly of a hog or tore up a horse's head. Like when a dog went mad and Daddy leaned the stock of his .22 against his cheek and the gunpowder singed the air and the dog lay kicking on his side, confused that he couldn't move. Confused about the sudden ebbing of his spirit out of him. Sometimes when the screen door slammed, I would find a corner and curl up into a ball.

From the earliest age, I lived by ritual, and as I got older the rituals magnified. They held the world together, even though the world was still in a fog. They minimized the pain. Sit every day of summer and listen to the butterflies whisper. Touch the maple tree every spring morning. Bury eight circles of acorns at the edge of the woods every fall, one for each of us, and walk around the circles every Monday after school. Always carry a favorite rock, or piece of bark, or piece of wood in my pocket. Rub the dust off my yellow pencils every night before bed. Pray every night before bed. "Now I lay me down to sleep. I pray the Lord my soul to keep. Lord bless my family. Lord bless the grass. Lord bless the stars."

Be careful of what I touch. Because when I touch vinyl, a knife goes through my liver. When I touch concrete, cold hands wrap around my heart. "If you sit on concrete," the adults would say, "you get piles." Hogs with "piles" walked around with parts of their intestines, bright pink, hanging out of their rectums. When I touch wood, there is a soft humming. When I touch cold water, I drown. When I touch iron, I am crucified. Aluminum, I am ripped to shreds. Copper is a friendly hand, reaching out of water. When I touch polyester, my skin falls slowly apart, like filo burnt to a crisp. When

I touch glass, I get mildly shocked. When I touch hair, I'm inside someone else's body. When I touch grass, warm water runs over me. When I touch a blossom, I melt, dispelling my hunger. When I touch bark, I have déjà vus. When I touch mud, I am paralyzed, cold worms squirm inside me.

I was obsessed with light. I felt it as palpably as rain on my skin. If a room is too bright, get out of it. If I can't get out, find the shadow of a wooden object. If a room is too dim, close my eyes. The light has to have rose in it. It has to have indigo, diffused as the scent of earth after a summer shower, or I can't breathe. Then get out of it.

So much depended on me. Raise my hands to the windows three times each morning to let the slave children know I'm up. Call quietly to the sparrows four times, and then four times again, or the baby sparrows won't be able to fly. Tilt my head to the left at eleven o'clock so the clouds can drift left down the tilted sky. In the grayed, oak fence boards of the pigpen, there were eyes disguised as knots in the wood. Every day, brush my hands lightly over the eyes so that they will have sight and can look out at the garden and the orchard. Lightly, though, so that the boards won't be frightened and defend themselves with splinters. Every day, tap the corner of the henhouse so the chickens will keep laying. So the roosters will stay red. So the roosters will not turn entirely the green of one of their tail feathers.

Don't get up in the morning until I hear the pillows sigh. Touch each pillow five times or the pillows will cry. Whisper to them, because they like whispering. For some reason, I heard the cries of pillows more loudly than I heard those of anything else. They were like the whines of starving kittens, huddled together waiting for a mother that would never come back. And so, I had to mother them.

It took only small things to bring on a convulsion. Smells could trigger them. A wrong texture. A wrong sound. I hated nothing more than my convulsions. It wasn't so much the going as the coming back. I had seen other children with fits, and so I could imagine what I looked like. It was scary and grotesque, and the shame of wetting on myself, at whatever age I may have been, made me want to die. To just not exist.

Light breaking into the room the wrong way could trigger them. I had to always be in the right light, but never in the light entirely. Never so far away from shade that I couldn't reach out and hold on to it, leap back into it.

I was allergic to almost everything. But I wouldn't understand this until I was in my twenties and had moved away from home. The names of illnesses, such as "allergies," were not a part of my childhood. I was just "sick." I had severe reactions to dust, molds, pollens, animal hairs, feathers, water, vegetable and fruit skins. Bark. Metals. Insect bites and stings. I was stung so many times that it seemed like wasps hated me and sought me out. Wherever I was stung swelled quickly to many times its normal size. If I was stung anywhere on my face, my eyes would swell over until I was blind. If I was stung on a foot, I couldn't put on my shoe. I learned where the wasps hid: in sawdust, in bushes, in the eaves of houses, on the sides of boards, in holes in the ground. But there was no way to avoid all of these.

Sometimes Daddy took us to the CC camp, where the fresh scent of wood and sawdust was like a perfume, a liquor. I loved the feeling of sawdust under my feet, the whirring sound of saw blades singing in the sun, the glistening skin of dark sweaty men, and the bowed and straight long lengths of brown and pink cedar planks, edged with gray bark. But almost always while I was there, I'd step on a nest of wasps, and red, black, and yellow, they'd sting me with a fury.

I was having asthma attacks all the time and almost dying. Each spring, when the wild onions shouted through the ground and the jonquils opened and spewed their pollens to the winds, when the bees hummed like twisters around the dazzling forsythia and the dogwoods splayed open in mock stigmatas, I took a deep breath and felt my chest closing. I could feel the mindful spreading of toxins through my lungs, like bony fingers, like spider web, like deer sinew being pulled tight around a pelt. I could feel the breath leaving me, refusing to return, my chest tightening as if someone was turning a wrench, and the sound of my wheezing and labored breath as abrupt as the caw of crows in early dawn. People say that life is free, but it didn't feel that way to me. I had to work hard to stay alive.

I was often saying goodbye to the people looking down at me, whose fear I could smell, who seemed to also be saying goodbye to me. Daddy would sit by the bed sometimes and hold my hand. "Dennis, do you feel like you're dying?" he'd ask, almost reverently. "No, Daddy, no, I'm not dying," I'd reassure him.

I often had a knot in my stomach, a sinking feeling. Almost nothing was clear. Sometimes people were so nice to me that the knot disappeared. Sometimes I could run and play with my brothers and sisters and cousins from through the woods, and I would know what I was doing. And I could even come out first, or on top, or win. Sometimes my body could do the right things, as good as, or better than, some of the others.

The times when I could run and play would never last long. Something not human would come and get me. *Where am I going when I'm not here anymore?* I wondered a lot, lying in bed. *What will it be like? Who will be my mama there? Will it hurt?* "Will it hurt?" I asked the tall shadow in the corner of the room, as filaments of dust floated in the small light from the window. "Is my baby brother there? Will I see him? Will he know me?" Some days the shadow stayed put, silent, present, but not really watching me. Some days he lifted up his head and opened a trembling mouth filled with sharp teeth. Other days, there was a glow, like that from the sun, but not really, because it was strangely made of something unlike light, which I never quite understood. "Can you play with me?" I asked on some days, and he would. He took me places filled with the music of waterfalls, through layers of gauze and fog. He took me to meadows where no sound could be heard, and we played hide-and-seek among stones that were soft when I fell. He took me to places where the moonlight touched and held me and the sobs that wracked my body moved away from me, rippling the very atmosphere, where my breath made the wind that rustled the leaves and my tears flew into the clouds like birds with a single mind.

I never really wanted to talk, but I didn't want to be what my parents called "retarded." I heard them sometimes, talking about me. They said maybe I was the sign of their sins, and I didn't want to be their sins. If I were their sins, I could never go anywhere, or ride in a car or on a bus. Like my cousins across the road, and my other cousin down in the bottom, I would always have to stay at home.

So I tried to try. I opened my mouth and tried to speak but could only grunt. I watched my mama and my granny's mouths closely, but after a few words, my attention would wander to the shapes of their teeth, the little holes on their tongues, or the sounds of other things, like my baby sister crying, a rooster, a cow, the dogs.

I tried to stop tasting people, and talk, because it bothered people. I tasted them as a natural reflex, the way animals did. At first with my real tongue, slyly, holding on to someone's arm. And then with some other tongue no one could see. I tasted what was in their cells with a warm curiosity. I smelled them and listened to their footsteps and the way they breathed.

By the time I was four, when the first words spilled out, my parents had almost given up. When I was older, they would laugh about all the pig and cow grunts I made, the new languages I taught them. But back then, they worried. But talking would never come easy. It would never feel natural. I felt as if words were stones attached to threads of my body. As soon as they left my mouth, they sank into invisible waters, slowly unraveling the spools of my belly and heart.

Certain sounds caught my ear, and so I made them over and over. Car. Car. Car. Car. Car. Car. Car. Car. Car. Car. Car. Car. Car. "Put that plate on the kitchen counter, Bubba." Put that plate. Put that plate. Put that plate. Put that plate. Put that plate. Put that plate. Put that plate . . . Sometimes the sounds startled me, because they seemed to be coming from somewhere else, from someone other than me. Sometimes my brothers and sisters would complain.

"Mama, can you make Dennis stop!?" "All right, Red," my mama would say. And I would keep rocking to the sound, back and forth, back and forth, sitting there on the floor, or the bed, but only whispering now. My mama and my daddy called me "Red" because my hair turned fiery in the sun. All right, Red. All right, Red. All right, Red. All right, Red. All right, Red. All right, Red. I couldn't stop the repeater. And not repeating was like not shivering when it was freezing cold.

And this was the thing about talking. Some of the parts of me that are most me have still never talked. They can't. I don't know exactly how to explain it. If I was sitting in a room sorting rocks, or pieces of bark, or lost in splotches of light, or reading a book and someone came in and started talking, a part of me might turn and say something to them. It might say something and then say something else. But a part of me would keep its back turned. It couldn't help it.

The me I knew best listened. I was the child who lay awake at night, listening. I was the child who stayed behind at the dinner table when all the other children had gone, listening to my mama and daddy and sometimes my granny talk, slowly sorting my food and planning combinations of bites. I was the child in my mama and daddy's bed. They talked at night, and I listened. In the sounds of their breathing as they slept were cities filled with restless and hungry people. The sounds of their talking were my blankets. The colors their talking made were my pillows. Sometimes their talking was a growing mass of crisscrosses, green like the holly. Other times the threads went through me, like swords, and twisted together, like roots going through earth.

But there were plenty of other people talking all around me, a matrix of talk. So no one missed my voice. And I was listening to spirits. Behind my granny's house, in the meadow where my birth trailer had been, were locust trees. There were other trees whose names I do not know. And in the meadow the spirits came and went. There was Grandpa Walter, Cousin Molly, Great-great-grandmother, Hattie, Gracie, Ophelia, Nathaniel, Douglass, and many others. Pods fell from one of the trees and burst open, seeds singing with souls from another era. On the borders of the meadow were my granny's flowerbeds, filled with roots and bulbs. And all of them knew the spirits. Snow on the mountain. Begonias. Pansies. Daffodils. Madonna lilies. I could hear spirits moving across the hydrangeas, the papery lips of gladiolus, sweet peas, and impatiens.

Alongside the meadow, across a little fence, was a road that went back through the woods. A lot of our cousins lived back through there. I could hear them talking through the thick cluster of woods. Yelling out. Laughing. Our cousins' mama was named Betty and their daddy's name was Nat. Our cousins were named Freda, Lynn, Bootsie Lee, Man, and Baby Sis. I could hear them talking sometimes, coming and going, passing by our house. Sometimes we took the rutted path through the woods, going to our cousins' house. The path went down a hill where, at the bottom, a wooden bridge passed over a small creek, and then gradually climbed and curved around to right. Some days we went to their house, and some days they came to ours. Their house was small, the boards warped and gray, their grain washed rough by decades of weather. They were ashy, like our bony black arms and legs. You would never want to run your bare skin along them, for fear of getting splinters. Sometimes we played in the woods or fields, and other times we played in their yard and ours, where dogs and cats and chickens ran freely about.

Mama and Granny and Daddy talked about our cousins sometimes. They were "good time" people, they said. But our family didn't understand the idea of a good time. It puzzled us. Good time went with not getting ahead, and so we condemned it. We were "church people." Good time was devil things. Good time was sin. On Saturday nights our cousins drank and laughed, juked, smoked, danced, and planted sloppy kisses all over each other's good-time bodies. Or so we were told. And so it was often with a long, stern eye on us that our parents said, "I guess so" when we asked to go through the woods to our cousins' house and play.

My uncle T lived with my cousins, and he would walk over to Granny's to visit us. Uncle T was one of the old, old folks. He was born with feet that couldn't sit flat, and so he walked on his toes. He took care of a lot of children, and grandchildren, cooking and cleaning. He chopped wood, sitting down. I remember the light around his beautiful black face. He hobbled with his twisted walking stick, humming, singing, or just making a grunting noise to himself that old people sometimes made. He sat on Granny's porch and talked to her. I sat playing in the sand. He talked to me. He could really see me. He teased me and laughed. He called me "Denny Flootie Boots" and "Denny Wheatstraw." I remember his baggy old brown pants and his red Prince Edward tobacco cans. The way he seemed to be dancing slowly, even when he was just standing there talking. I remember his suspenders and swollen knuckles wrapped around the wood of his walking cane. I remember the music of his talk. I remember his pure love.

Not far from our cousins' house was Grandma Addie's, our daddy's grandmother. She was half Mattaponi, a Native American tribe. She was very light skinned with straight white hair. She had hairs growing on her chin and always had an apron on. She'd come out in the yard when she heard us approaching. "Come on in here, chirren," she would say sometimes and usher us in and give us a little treat. Her house smelled of firewood and cedar and cooking grease.

Then there were all the other cousins on the other side of the road, also going farther and farther back through the woods. When I was little, children and grown-ups would be coming and going all the time. People would just show up and shout out, "Comin' in!" when arriving at each other's door, just before entering. People would be yelling out, carrying all sorts of things on the wind, the way Africans had, the way the slaves had. I never really had to talk.

But as we got older, history would drift over us and shower us with yellow pollen, and like that, we would be changed. What had held us all together in slavery days, and in the decades afterward, would drift away from us, would get lost with the memories and the passing of the old people. The horses and the cows would die, and we wouldn't get new ones. One morning, all of the chickens would have disappeared. One day, we would be eating the last bacon from the smokehouse, and there wouldn't be any more pigs. The fruit and berry orchards would grow over with stubble and weeds. The fields of corn would no longer turn the light green.

People's voices would stop ringing out in the woods or across fields. We would start to get modern. News would stop being carried through shouts. The naked shouts of day-to-day feelings would wither like plants pulled from a garden. The bare songs of people walking, or digging, or cutting wood, or feeding pigs, or calling cows, would stop. When I was little, people's voices were as thick as those of crickets and frogs and owls and whippoorwills and cicadas.

But a deafening silence would come, replaced by the noise of a red radio. I desperately wanted to smash the red radio, to play with shattered pieces of its hardened plastic. But each time I got near it, it would whisper. It would hypnotize me with its perfectly square corners. With its perfect symmetry. Even if it wasn't turned on. And if it was turned on, I wouldn't dare approach it. The way its indifferent spirit bent around corners and spilled beneath the crack of the closet door as I hid inside, sprawled in piles of dirty laundry, frightened me and kept me at bay.

People didn't know it, but the animals and plants had been helping to tell our stories. We would come to a moment when the young people wouldn't know the little stories, they knew only the big one. The little stories would be lost somewhere in our hearts, somewhere in houses in our bodies. But we couldn't get to them. The stories were dancing on the tongues of spirits, but most of us couldn't hear them. In that new age, we would close our doors to each other, unless there were emergencies. We would not want each other to know what things we had gotten, or not gotten, from the white world to put in our houses. We would start collecting white objects. Suddenly, we would be told not to go into anyone else's houses anymore, and our cousins would no longer be allowed to enter ours.

I was in love with the beauty of my family and my cousins. The forms and the tones of their bodies. From the darkest, blueish-black skin to the lightest. From the nappiest hair to the straightest. With the way they talked. They oozed a sweetness. A distinct flavor that I can still taste if I close my eyes. That flavor was my spirit. That flavor was my body. Growing up, I thought that I would always be surrounded by it. That we would all live there, in the Body, forever. That's how it had always been, for most of us. In that body, I did not have to explain anything. I could communicate and not have to talk. People just understood what I was feeling.

But when history changed us, that's when I really started to talk. I was trying to bring the sweetness back. I was trying to hold on to things. Being sweet was a big thing for people where I lived. Sweet was good hearted. Sweet was mannered. Sweet was kind. Sweet was the blood that spilled from you if you were cut open. Sweet held me like a second mama. My daddy would always say to me, from the time I was a baby, until I was fifty, when he died, "Always stay sweet, Red." I still find myself liking people better if they are sweet. When I talk, I am still chasing sweetness like a butterfly following the color of a blossom.

The Big Yellow Bus

A picture is worth a thousand words.

The first day of school, my mama dropped me off and left. I don't know how we got there, since we had only one car and Daddy had taken it to work. Daddy and cars went together. He had an old blue DeSoto. Blue like a bird's egg. When Daddy sat in his DeSoto, he almost disappeared, he was so blue. But he was a darker blue than the DeSoto. I remember him pulling out of the yard one day. Yellow bells blooming. Jonquils. White dogwood blossoms. One puff of white clouds in a still blue sky. A sky that was swallowing up time. And there was dark-blue Daddy in a light-blue DeSoto, the window rolled down, waving as he pulled out of the driveway.

One minute I was standing in the yard, holding rocks and sticks, floating on clouds in a blue sky, and the next minute I was riding in a car, talking to Jeremiah. *I think we're going to Ashland, Jeremiah. Mama seems worried, but I don't know why.* And then I was holding Mama's hand and we were walking into a building where other children were playing and crying. Mama was talking to some women, and then she was gone. At first I thought she was coming back because she had never left me anywhere, other than at home.

Before we started school, none of my brothers or sisters had ever been beyond the safety of our community for any length of time. In those days there was no such thing as kindergarten; we just went into first grade. We had ridden into Ashland on Saturdays to go shopping for groceries, ice, livestock feed, and salt blocks for the cow. Sometimes we stayed in the car while Mama shopped for groceries in Crosses, the small local market that offered credit to black families. There was still segregation then. I think that Daddy and Mama wanted to shield us from the world, from the demeaning glares of white people, from the bowing and deferential manners that black people masked themselves in when interacting with whites. If we knew anything as children, we knew that the outside world was not safe.

When I realized that Mama had left me, I thought I would never stop crying. Even when I did stop, I soon started again, triggered by the cries of others around me. As terror overcame me, I fell from weeping into quiet despair, into paralysis.

When the teacher picked me up, I was already seeing nothing. She talked to me and she talked to me. She talked to me in a quiet voice. And once I looked at her, when she wasn't looking at me. I sat close to her and searched for Mama in her voice, in her smell, in the gentleness of her movements.

After that first day, the big yellow bus would barrel down the rutted dirt road every morning, coming to get us. Like sacrificial lambs, we walked blankly into her hungry mouth and sat down in her belly. Strung together by invisible chains, we felt ashamed and defeated. We stoically paraded on board the ship and waved goodbye to our home.

For a year I rode the bus with just my older brother, Richie. I rode with my eyes closed, gripping the cool, round metal on the side of the seat, next to the wall. I was so nowhere that I remember little of it. The next year my sister, Elaine, started school, and so then there were three of us. But again, I remember little of it. The next year my youngest brother, Levi, started school. I remember the driver's name was sometimes Mrs. Chaney and sometimes Mrs. Lewis, both heavy-set black women who had children around our ages. They were stern and motherly. The seats were hard and cold. The roar of the bus engine scared me. There were angry people being ground up over and over under the yellow hood. There was a smell of burning oil, almost sweet. By the second year I kept my eyes open and let them go blank in the blur of passing cars and trees. I sank my fingers into the music of the black tires singing. Sometimes I closed my eyes when the bus turned. I liked the turns. They made my body laugh and laugh. Sometimes I closed my eyes and rode my yellow bulldozer, my black train, my red dump truck, all the way to school.

Our school was John M. Gandy, the only black school in the area. But that wasn't its original name. In the period after slavery, it had been Hanover County Training School. My mama had gone there, after going for years in the little one-room schoolhouse out by our church. I wonder what Mama felt like when she first went to school. How did she get there? She never looks happy in the few black-and-white pictures we have of when she was a little girl. She's never smiling. She looks sad. She looks like she's already learned just to do what she has to do.

That one-room schoolhouse my mama went to first was built for the children on the plantation. It still sits there, beside our church. When I was around ten, I would go in there sometimes and play on an old abandoned organ. Most of the floor was covered with stacks of yellowed newspaper. Light spilled in through cracks in the wall, and I could hear the buzzing of dirt daubers and red wasps. If we were city people, and if we weren't all neurologically challenged. If we had recovered enough from our shell shock to organize. To get signatures and get it in the newspaper. Those kinds of things. I suppose the schoolhouse would be a historic property by now. I suppose we would have petitioned the town and written letters. We would have rallied public support. But we hadn't. We are still astonished just to be alive. To have the liberty to own houses, drive cars, go shopping in white stores, wear good clothes, watch television. To curl up on a couch or bed, pull the blanket up, and exhale.

At Gandy everybody, all day, every day, was black. Our teachers were educated, but we still recognized them as us. However strange sitting still and saying nothing may have been, someone like us was there to soften the strangeness of it. They talked to us as one of us, even when they spoke "proper."

Growing up, we had never sat down at a desk; in fact, we didn't own one. There were no spaces in our house for printed pages, for writing or reading. The shapes that the body gets into when the eyes are feasting on print were foreign and uncomfortable. Just to sit up straight in a chair all day, or to bend over a table for hours, was hard. What to do with the motion in our bodies? It was daytime, but we had to put our bodies half to sleep, to contort them and hold them like little Houdinis.

There were a few books in our house, some that my mama had when she was a girl, with yellowed and brittle pages. Pictures of Mary and her little lamb. Words my mama had written in cursive on delicate paper. My mama's writing was so pretty. It flowed like waves of music. It led like blue-lit tunnels under oceans, through forests, invisibly through cities. It came off the page and touched me.

The first words I learned to read, I think, were "Consider goat!" (which I pronounced "con cider"). They were printed beneath a picture in one of those books. In the black-and-white picture, a little white boy is yelling at a stubborn goat. He has a string around the goat's neck and is pulling him in one direction while the goat is trying to go in another. The book was on a shelf in the living room. I crawled from cold linoleum to warm, soft beige carpet to get to the shelf. There was a red piece of knitting across the arm of the couch that I lost my face in, like a diver breaking the surface loses himself in oxygen. I have moments now when I find that same piece of knitting. The way shadows change the colors of material in a store. In the color in someone's house. At home. "Con cider, goat," the boy was saying. "Con cider!"

I couldn't read the rest of the story, but I could fill it in. The boy's mama had told him to take the goat out to the field and tie him to a stake so that he could graze. But the boy had spent too much time thinking about taking the goat. He had spent too much time standing in the shade with the goat. Him and the goat, standing in the shade, watching the spirits playing. By the time he had remembered he was supposed to be taking the goat, a group of spirits had gathered in the field. They were having a big meeting.

Everything went fine leading the goat halfway across the clearing. But when they got to the field of spirits, it was another story.

"Con cider!" meant I'm sorry. I don't want to leave you either, but what choice do I have? "Con cider!" meant please, for my sake, do it even if it hurts.

I felt so awkward in school. The classrooms were so open and bright. The bells exploded in my belly and made me want to puke. The long hallways were cool, and quiet, but somehow menacing. There was no space to catch up with my breath. My fire burned out before the day was over. It went dim in the face of all the brightness, motion, and noise. I tried in many ways to hold on to it. I held my breath as if I was sinking under water. I crossed my feet under the desk, as if I had to pee. I walked slowly, as if I was carrying a plate balanced on my head. I was silent. But nothing helped. There was nowhere to go to feel things. There was nowhere to hear the spirits. And how could I survive without my things? How could I stay upright all day without a soft thing to hold, to lean against, a pillow to talk to? I could feel myself disappearing, like sand out of a hole in a crocus bag, as the hands of the big clock over the teacher's desk tick-tocked relentlessly. At school, whoever I really was, fled so far away even I could never find him.

But I had to go to school. Mama said so. This was what the slaves had fought for.

Things were quieter in the classroom than they were outside, in the cafeteria, or in the halls, but they were never truly quiet. The hum of the florescent lights was like the roar of an engine. I kept waiting for other kids to seem bothered by it, but no one ever was. The ticking of the clock was like knives slicing through my brain. I couldn't hear the butterflies. I couldn't find Jeremiah.

At recess, I huddled near the building, touching the wall for security, watching the other children yell and fight and run and throw balls. There was a tall spirit under the sycamore tree outside. Sometimes I talked with him. Sometimes he took me into the tree, which was like a soft room with no clouds. I could walk out of that room into a meadow of singing sparrows. I could hover and glimmer like heat rising from August asphalt. And no one could see me. The spirit's name was William. I was never as close to William as I was to Jeremiah, but I looked forward to seeing him. He was older and spoke sometimes as if he was talking to himself, even when he was looking at me. And I could only see him sometimes, because he couldn't go any farther than the shade of the tree's branches. When it rained, I gazed out of the window as water dripped from the leaves, washing away all shadows, and wondered what William was doing.

The one thing that happened, that made me feel like I was part of everybody else, was when the boxer Muhammad Ali came to our school. He came because we were black. But I don't know how he knew about us, or how he got there. Excitement and pride swept through the hallways and under the doors of classrooms until everyone had to open their doors. We spilled out into the street, where he joked and played and punched the air and picked a small child up and smiled at him. Before I knew it, we were all a parade, heading down the street, surrounding him. We passed by the black bakery we were forbidden to go to during school hours. The sweet scent made us drunk. We passed the black funeral home with the somber black hearse. Watching Muhammad Ali that day, I learned to joke with a straight face. I became Mr. Laughter, but hardly anybody knew. Hardly anybody got it.

People thought so differently at school. Instead of letting things come to them, sifting through invisible threads, they went out and attacked things and then dragged them back home. There was never time to wait. They shot thoughts and tied them on the rooftops of cars and trucks. People outside our tribe were hunters. People in my tribe were gardeners and carpenters. They grew things. They built things from visions. I had to learn to hunt if I wanted to live in the world, whether I liked it or not. But hunting made me nauseous. I could never kill things. I could never cut their throats and bleed them. And so I tied them up and dragged them home. Or I bribed them with candy or biscuits, or a promise of giving them something that they longed for. Math problems longed for square boxes, to hold them in place. The names of countries longed for vitamin C, and so I promised them oranges. But things I bribed or dragged home were never happy, and they usually didn't stay for very long. They stayed just long enough for me to pass tests, to say goodbye, and to ask if they would come back sometime if I needed them.

I had an insatiable appetite for learning and for "getting" things, and *A*'s came easily. But it wasn't the actual information that usually captured and fascinated me. It was the beauty of how things had been ordered, organized, named. Someone had taken the time to give names to the millions of animals and plants. To the planets and stars. To the clouds. Someone had mapped out how the sky fit together into constellations. The parts of the body, inside and out. The bodies of land and water. Mountains. The shapes of things. The metals and stones and gems. The seasons. Someone had split the world in half and named the hemispheres. Angles. And the names were all so beautiful. So mysterious. Orion. The Himalayas. The Amazon. The Red Sea. Circles. Trapezoids. Stamen. Amoeba. Retina. It made the world less overwhelming, safer. It told me that there were people like me, who had spent most of their time paying close attention to the nature of the world, thinking about and organizing things.

Unlike most others around me, though, I never took the knowledge as real or absolute. I knew that to get a good grade, I needed to remember things and put them down on paper. I knew that getting a good grade was important. Adults liked you better if you got good grades. It made them happy. But I fit the information into my private world.

I considered almost everything I learned in school to be made up, and I made up my own parallels. It was one of the things that made learning so much fun. I remembered things by remembering what I made of them. The stars were babies trapped in the milky darkness of space. Someone had given them names to be nice, to hold them in place for us to name them for ourselves. Venus was my cousin Betty Rose. The skeleton system was the oak at the edge of the woods. The western hemisphere was the nearby town of Ashland.

Stamens were the yellow ribbons in Janet Jones's hair. When we learned to tell time, twelve o'clock was the chimney of an old house that had fallen down in the woods, a long walk from our house. It whispered and was full of spirits. The woods were full of old wells, and China was a well that Beulah saved me from falling in. England was another well. No matter what the teacher said about the clock, or what I wrote down on papers, I knew that there was no quarter past or half past. There was twelve, and then vapors. The time was something someone else made up, and so I could also make up my own, one that would suit me better.

I had trouble with time, with what people called minutes, or hours, or days. There could be a lot of minutes in what people called a minute, depending on what was happening. It wasn't a short thing at all. The same thing with hours and days. If I was trying to put my shoes on and somebody yelled hurry up and the birds were asking me to listen and the things on the bed weren't straight and the pillows were moaning and the water inside my body was sloshing from side to side as if I was on a boat and I started to cry and get maddened and then my head caught on fire, I couldn't see anything anymore and I didn't know where I was. I wanted to scream at somebody and hurt somebody or break something against the wall to reset the day. And then my mama might come in the room and say, "Red, we need to leave soon. Just take your time and put your shoes on, honey." Mama's voice and her not yelling would stop time. And then I wouldn't hear anything at all. And I would be exhausted, like at bedtime, but it wouldn't be night yet. I would put my shoes on, and I would wash my face, and I would straighten out the things on my bed, and I would hug my pillows. And then it would be a different day, but people would say that it was still Monday.

2 + 2. But what is 2? Where is it?

"D-o-g" spells dog. But "dog" isn't a real dog. "Dog" is a word someone made up. So why can't "d-o-g" spell cat, if you want it to?

I learned to grow masks for school. I had to be careful there. Covering up was like instinct, though. Like a brown walking stick turning green when it sits on a leaf. Watch. Watch. Watch. Watch hands. Watch lips. Watch eyebrows. Watch the paths that come down beside noses and curve out and around. I grew masks like extra thumbs. Like a flower sprouting the wrong blossoms. I had learned a lot from insects about how to live around people. I had learned a lot from growing up in the shadow of slavery. Slaves had to have six senses. They had to pay attention to small things, to small routines, to other people's view of things. They were always strangers, ready for the next trauma.

But sometimes at school, I forgot to cover up. Mostly after naptime. My favorite time in elementary school was naptime. I could lay my head on the desk and cover my ears with my arms, fall asleep, and be back at home. I could feel for a little while that I was not yet split apart.

At naptime I often dreamed about my mama and my granny back at home. The green grass in our yard. The birds talking to each other in the damson plum trees. Mama was hanging out clothes, and I was standing beside her, holding on to her apron. I awoke from my nap, laughing and talking to Mama. When I realized where I was, and that others had already awoken and had heard me, I felt as embarrassed as I did in dreams when I went to school in my pajamas.

At school, we were supposed to just see things like looking across the surface of a lake. We weren't supposed to dive or float, just keep looking across. When people talked to us, I was supposed to look at them and just see the surface of their faces. Not even that, really. Because I wasn't supposed to notice the lines, or spots, the moles, dislocations, textures, or asymmetries. I was supposed to just hear their words and to believe them.

But I found doing these things very difficult. I wanted to listen to people's bodies and their spirits. I wanted to look at them without the awkward, burning pain of them looking back. I had no interest in their words the way they meant them. So often they seemed to mean something else anyway. I was interested in the sounds they made when they spoke. In their smells, in their movements. Sometimes I frightened other children when I looked intensely at them. It made them uneasy. They sometimes joked with each other about my weirdness, wondering what I was looking at.

"Today, class, we're going to work on writing."

"Robert, stop that talking. Janet, stop writing on your desk. Pencils down, please. Pencils down, please! I don't think I said anything about picking pencils up, did I?"

Silence . . .

"Did I!?"

"No, ma'am."

"All right, then." More silence as she sternly looks over the classroom, making sure she has everyone's total attention. "Now you may open your notebooks. Do it without talking, please. Without talking."

I focused hard on my teacher, Mrs. Roberts. I learned her. I was used to watching, listening from the shadows, and learning people. I watched everything, or at least the things that I found most fascinating or necessary for survival. The leaves of plants. The looks in animals' eyes. The way they moved. How they regarded other species. Spiders. Wasps. Clouds. Mama. Daddy. Sisters and brothers. When I was young, I didn't think of people as different from other things. I didn't quite get that I was one of them. When Mrs. Roberts talked to the class, the sound of her words was gray, like the gray sound of a heavy oak desk sliding across the tiled floor. No wonder she was tired by the end of the day. When she talked to me, though, the sound of her words was like the color of pink hibiscus.

Before long, I knew what my teacher would say and when she would say it. I learned to always keep one eye and one ear open for my teacher. At the same time, though, I folded myself into an origami kite and flew above the trees, landing in green places, and with my other eye I watched blues and greens go by. With my other ear, I rode waves of sound, far and near. Someone yelling down the street. Someone talking in the hall. The giant arm of a garbage truck straining to lift and bend itself into a half moon. Birds. Oh, the birds! A door slamming.

If my teacher had sweat on her forehead, she would be stern. If there were fine beads of sweat gathered on her fleshy brown arms, in the stretch marks, she would smile at me and touch my head. If the scent of her perfume was thick, like women in church, she would speak in all declaratives. If she looked out the window a lot, she would shower us with interrogatives. "Did I say anything about talking?" "Did I ask anyone to write on the board?" "Did I tell anybody they could leave yet?"

I watched and listened when she and the other teachers would whisper. Sometimes they whispered about kids and laughed at them. I wondered if she ever laughed at me. I knew that she liked rose-scented lotion and that she pulled it from her desk drawer whenever there was a recess and spread it on her arms and hands. I knew that breathing roses made her feel better. Breathing roses made me feel better too. So after recess I always got as close to her as I could, walking slowly, getting happy. I knew when her mind wandered, like Mama's did sometimes. I knew when she worried. When she was happy. When she was happy she gave off soft breezes. I knew when she was sad. When she was sad she gave off too much heat. She felt like fire.

I sat in hard chairs at school and half listened. I could figure out how to do most things before the teacher finished explaining them. Then I could daydream. I watched the other kids and learned them. I found my groove. The ideal spots. I was fine as long as nothing disrupted the daily routine. As long as no one bothered me. Although a headache was always right around the corner, hovering above me, like a cloud. I loved my fat, yellow pencil and the big lines on easily torn pages of paper. I loved my notebook. My eraser. My crayons. My cubby. My old, worn wooden desk. I loved them partially because I had to, though. They were what I was left with, away from home.

I loved my shoes. My clothes. I loved having them. I loved the idea of being a person, but I loved it partially because I had to. Until first grade, we never really had many "nice" clothes. Not that we had a lot of them once we started school. But school brought a sense of "mine-ness" that I had never felt much. At home I was just a limb of a whole body. People seemed to see the five kids as one person with five heads. Even my mama and daddy, sometimes. Everyone had trouble telling me and my brothers apart. We wore the same clothes. We were always together. The inch difference in our heights was our only separation. We were taught to always think of ourselves as one thing, that thinking about our separate selves was selfish. We were the "Follys," and we were proud of it.

A few rows back from the teacher's desk, near the window, was the best spot in the classroom. I could bask in the openness of seasonal skies and feel the fall, spring, and early summer breezes that blew in the window. I could smell the leaves and grass, jonquils or rained-on earth, doughnuts baking at the bakery down the street. The sounds of other children, passing cars, and conversations of teachers who stood against the wall to talk at recess or when their classes were having PE settled in my ears. I could see Jeremiah waiting for three o'clock, when I could come home. In many ways, school was like water over a duck's back. I mastered it. I grew to love its structure, routine, and safety. I grew to love Janet Jones's smile and her light-brown upper arm. Sometimes when my head ached or when my stomach was sinking so fast I couldn't breathe, I stared at her arm to feel better. But school didn't sink into me very deeply. My soul still lingered at home, in the house and in the synapses of my family and kin.

I remember looking so forward to learning to write in cursive. It was so pretty. So magical and secret. It was like the curves in flowers, in someone's song or dance. But I missed those weeks from school when they were learning cursive. I was so sad. It was like missing the flocks of canaries when they passed through in the spring, and for moments the trees were filled with delicate, yellow flecks, and the air was filled with a light, sweet singing. Weeks went by in bed, in and out of delirium. In and out of time, as Mama and Granny's voices were the touchstones, and my brothers' and sisters' clatter, like light and dark, sunshine and starlight, came and went. This was the way it was. I would go to school for a little while, and then I would get sick again and disappear.

Going to the Moon

Rule number 33: Never let people know that objects are alive.

By the time I was eleven, my clairvoyance heightened. If someone was going to pass away, I could feel it. If someone was coming. If someone was going to have a baby. If someone was going to be in an accident. I knew too much. I still felt too much. If it was going to rain in one or two days, I could feel the air shifting. It tilted my bones. It moved the light to a different part of the yard, from the begonias to the shade beneath plum trees. But the shade wouldn't budge for anything, and so the light was hiding now, the way the shade often did. Everything turned maroon. The water dropped two degrees inside of me, and so I huddled inside, even though everybody said, "But it's so warm!" I could smell the coolness of the rain days before it came, me and the cows and dogs.

I was still sick a lot, but not as much. I didn't miss as much school. I could feel sick but still manage to do things sometimes. I still cried a lot, but my body didn't jerk as much from the smells and sounds of things or from too much light. I still sulked, and I was still prone to long silences and meltdowns. I still missed a lot of what was going on with people, but I laughed more, even at things that others didn't think were funny. I laughed a lot to myself, at people. How they were. How little sense they made. I started to become more aware of my difference and to resent people, to hold the harshness of the world against them.

I began to notice the people around me. I started trying to be more of a person. I started to like school. To feel safe there. Before then, I had been mostly waiting to die. I was like a traveler stranded in a foreign airport, absorbed with the strangeness of everything around me. I still looked into the sky a lot and imagined a ship would someday be coming. My favorite book was *You Will Go to the Moon*. In the book, a boy is taking a journey into space on a rocket ship, stopping off at a space station and then continuing on to the moon. I read it over and over, spending hours just looking at the pictures and imagining I was the boy. I read it even when I was older. I dreamed of being inside the space station, which was round, like a giant doughnut, turning ever so slowly, a muted carousel among the stars. It must be so quiet and cozy in the spaceship, in dark space among the planets.

I would meet other beings in space who would be like me, who would talk to me like plants or spirits, without any words. The way flowers talk, quietly humming. The way the stars talk, with patterns of light. Beings who would not look at me. Who would just do whatever they were doing, and I could do whatever I was doing. And there wouldn't be any hurry or any time. And that would be all right.

My other favorite books were about nature, and about a boy with an animal who was his best friend, like *Old Yellow* or *Black Stallion*. One whole set of books was all about the animal kingdom, and another was all about the plant kingdom. They were small books, about five-by-seven inches, with lots of pictures, and they fit perfectly in my hands. They don't make books like those anymore. The pages were slick and shiny and felt good to touch. Light would bounce off of the pages when I turned them and take me in. The colors were so deep they came alive. I would carry one of the books around with me or fall asleep with one of them next to my head. It was fun deciding which one to carry on any given day. There were so many beautiful rules for deciding. If Mama cooked bacon for breakfast, carry the book with butterflies. If Daddy talked to Mama before leaving, carry the book with fruit trees. If my sister Jean said something to my sister Thelma and she laughed, and then the man on the radio said something with three words with long *e*'s, carry the book of lizards and snakes. Sometimes deciding was as much fun as carrying or reading the books.

The six volumes about animals were about reptiles, insects, mammals, birds, fish, and amphibians. Along with the color photographs of each type of animal was information about them. Birds and insects were probably the dearest to my heart, and then amphibians and mammals. I spent days reading and gazing at the photographs, studying every detail, trying to absorb their spirits.

I spent days searching for animals, watching them, getting to know them, losing track of time. I was fascinated with how they ate; how they drank; how they moved their heads, their tails, wings, legs, mouths; how they stayed still. With what their sense of the minutes, hours, and days might be. With what kinds of houses they built. With when and how they slept, and what textures and colors they liked most. With how they regarded the other lives around them, especially people.

Of all the insects, wasps, bees, hornets, and yellow jackets seemed to be the most aware of people and to dislike us the most. Them, and the arachnids. Spiders watched us. I could feel their stares. Some of them might back up when people came along, but even then they never conceded. Bees lived in a world that floated somewhere in another dimension, in a forest or a field we never went into or ever touched. According to their laws, a few of them come into our world, but not many. They never let us know where they lived, how many of them there were, or what they were like when they were at home.

There was an ongoing war between us and wasps. If they built nests around the house eaves, or in the corners of the outhouse, or in the chicken coop, the barn, or in hedges near the house, Daddy would take a cup of kerosene and douse them. Then we'd run as the gasoline dripped from the nest and the wood it hung from, and they came furiously buzzing out, looking for someone to sting. Every time I got stung, I could feel their hate and anger. I could feel them saying, "Why don't you creatures go back to where you came from!?"

I loved praying mantises for the sheer beauty of their color, for the way they clung almost frozen to the branches of hedges. For the way they moved so slowly and the way they used their eyes to sense as much as they used them to see. They were like little dinosaurs, still recovering from the ice age, slowed to the speed of the sun, moving across the heavens.

Then there were the dirt daubers. If wasps were angry soldiers, dirt daubers were nervous sentries. They didn't fight. They watched out of the corners of their eyes, busily coming and going and adding bits of mud to their houses. I loved the black of their shiny, parchment-like blue-black wings with rainbows in them, like the blue-black of some chicken feathers. Their wings made me laugh. They were never still, moving rapidly, anxiously, even when they were not flying.

I kept a lot of insects and reptiles and amphibians for long enough to watch them, to listen to them and whisper to them. Then I would let them go. I had many turtles, snakes, tadpoles, and frogs. I kept them in crates and boxes I made from scrap wood and chicken wire, old pieces of glass and plastic and straw. I kept them in big jars. I kept them out behind the barn, on the shady side, unless the ground was damp—because I hated to walk on damp ground. Other times I moved them behind the back of the barn, facing the orchard and woods, where it was sunny.

I gathered the butterflies, ants, beetles, worms, mice, crickets, katydids, grasshoppers, and walking sticks in the boxes and jars near the house, or sometimes, if I could, I snuck them inside. I gathered them as carefully as Noah. I watched them to see if they would notice me, or if I was too big for their eyes, or if I was too small. I never tired of watching their movements and speeds, their angles and colors. They were often like nothing else on earth. A monarch's yellow is not the yellow of a canary. Is not the yellow of a daffodil. Is not the yellow of a primrose. Is not the yellow of a banana, or a yellow squash, or a tomato.

Colors vibrated. They rose like spirits of the dead and hovered around the thing. The hovering had ridges in it. The ridges around a katydid were nothing like those around a cornfield. Or those around asparagus, or a stem of wheat. They were not really like those around a blade of grass the katydids hid in, although they were much closer to those. That's how I found things so well, like green katydids in the grass, by looking at the ridges rather than at the colors.

I wanted to eat cicada songs. I wanted to retreat into some earlier form of life and enter the brown shells and exoskeletons they left gripping tree branches and fences, posts and leaves, stalks of tall grasses and mounds of earth. Whatever they left their shells on was suspended in time. When they sang, it felt like fields of a thousand ecstasies. Insistent. Urgent. As if life would end after each wave of singing gradually tapered off.

I didn't just keep the animals. I reveled in the feelings they gave me. I also gathered things that came from them. I thought the animals and the earth left them for me, like offerings to a friend, like gifts. I knew what "friend" meant. It meant someone who was nice to me, and life was nice to me, at least some of the time. It gave me sunshine. It gave me plants and animals, and they were nice to me in the feelings they gave me. I collected dirt dauber and wasp nests, cicada shells and dead cicadas, snakeskins, animal bones, teeth, tusks, claws, and spurs. Bodies and skeletons that had been hollowed out by ants. Things that didn't smell. I gathered wings. I kept pieces of butterfly wings I found in the grass.

I looked at bird wings in the woods, left over after a cat had eaten the bird. But I never kept one. They would bring bad luck. Feathers in a room would make the room move back and forth, and I would get nauseated. I kept birds' nests, though, abandoned in the spring for new ones. Nests kept the room warm, kept my spirit level. Some were made of thin twigs coiled around and woven together. Some were made of mud and twigs. Some had bits of plastic bags woven in. I was excited to find broken bird shells, imagining what it was like to be curled up inside one, to wake up and push out until the shell cracked open. They were so delicate and smooth. When I held them, their colors seeped into me.

The book set about the plant kingdom was also divided into several volumes. I was most interested in flowers and trees and all the magical things about them. Just reading some of the words and thinking about what they stood for was a kind of ecstasy. Reading "fruits," "seeds," "leaves," "stems," "blossoms," "pistil," "stamen," "pollen," "buds," and "roots" and looking at the pictures was like having Christmas morning, over and over and over. Reading "pollination" and "photosynthesis" made me giddy. Other words, like "mosses," "fungi," "bloom," "conifers," "algae," or "chlorophyll" were like the dark side of the moon, and so I avoided them, sped past them with eyes closed.

The faith of the seeds and bulbs amazed me. The idea that a seed could wait in the frozen ground, quietly, still, and alone, and then without looking know when it was time to sprout. That it knew when spring had come. That it could allow itself to rip open on the bottom, to burst again along an upper seam, and allow something delicate and albino to push upward, thirsty for a light it had never seen. I was also taken with the idea of forms. The idea that the bud would grow, that it would know what form to take. It would know whether to grow straight or tall, or to bend, or to curve, or to curl, or to twist. The idea that the stem would then grow buds and that, where once there was nothing, suddenly there were leaves. And the leaves knew what shapes to take, what colors. I loved the excitement of leaves, the way they loved the magic of sunlight that turned them green. And then there was all the magic of buds and blossoms. How they knew how to curl themselves and how they were sometimes more color and shape than they were matter.

I was especially excited about the tones and textures of leaves and stems. How there could be so many tones of green light and so many endless textures. When clover touched my skin, it reminded me of my mother's arm brushing against my face. The vines of morning glory made my body tingle. The color of their leaves in the early morning was like the C note on an oboe, and the blossoms swaying ever so slightly were like hypnotic splotches of light. The leaves of maples seemed to laugh and play like children, to take me up in them and float me on the wind. Poplars whispered. Cedars mourned. Pines did not want to be touched. The forsythia grew like baby fingers and could not stand straight for long under the weight of its own desires. Strawberry plants smelled me coming and got quiet. Blueberries never stopped talking. Blackberries were like old men, tired of the world, wanting to sink down into the thickets and explode with dark, ancient sweetness. I heard all the time from family and classmates and friends that I was in my own world. What they meant was that I wasn't in *their* world.

Seeds and pods were among my favorite things. Except in winter, we walked in a world of pods, and they were all different places with different personalities. There were distorted faces in the lily pods, faces of people who suffered for so long they were beyond us. When they burst open, they were like the bees. They were intensely into themselves, intently sending waves out to some force that remained hidden. The drum-head membranes of honesty pods also took on faces as spirits moved from one of them to another.

There were the startling white furs of milkweed pods that left an entire field near the woods rippling with eerie, otherworldly light. When they opened and the seeds started to crawl through gauze, the field became a sea, with mysterious creatures urgently moving in silent currents. I could hear moans, and I would never enter that field. If milkweed pods moaned and hissed like snakes do when people approach them, then thistles grimaced. They leapt onto my socks and onto the legs of my pants and tried to burrow into me.

Then there were the quiet orange pods of the silk tree. I could see the seeds plainly through the almost translucent skin. Sometimes they would open their eyes and catch me by surprise and then start laughing. Butterfly weed pods turned their heads and looked at me and then craned their necks upward, orange faces topped by silky white hair. They seemed to long for something in the heavens, to be calling out like a bird does when the eggs have been stolen from its nest.

Red maple pods filled the October air when wind blew, twirling downward like helicopters all around us. I picked them up and felt the bulge where the green let go of the stem and then brushed their fragile feather tips across my hands and cheeks. I washed myself in their odd magic until I could feel myself drifting through air. I flung them back into the sky, again and again, mesmerized by their spinning as they spiraled slowly down.

My favorite pods were those of the Kentucky coffee tree. There were two of them in Granny's front yard, near the wisteria arbor. The pods were dark brown and about two inches wide and sometimes eight inches long. If I picked the pods up at certain times and shook them, they *shhhhh*ed like maracas. But if I just held them long enough, they hummed, and although they seemed at first to be hardened ripples, they started to mold themselves into the palm of my hand. I sometimes pried them open at the seams. Inside, a perfect row of three to five black, kidney-shaped seeds lay suspended in a yellow, molasses-like gum.

I played games, like hide-and-seek, with the spirits in the pods. I talked to them. I didn't tell them my troubles, though. Because when I was sick or upset I didn't talk. And when I was talking I didn't remember I had troubles. By the time I was eleven, I no longer played games with spirits in pods as much, but I still talked to them. Some of my favorite ones were in special boxes in my room, like Uncle Tommy's Prince Edward cigar tins. But along with pods, I kept dried petals of flower blossoms that spirits liked. I liked handling them, how they dried to almost brittle but were still so full of energy. How it changed my hands to pick them up and hold them. I kept rocks with different textures and colors. I kept pieces of bark and stems, and pieces of sticks, usually ones that had faces in the grain or that seemed to hold a gesture I couldn't put my finger on, the feeling of motion.

Besides my spirit friends, and animal and plant friends, the wind and the clouds, my other best friend was a girl born prematurely with a boy attached to her at the hips. Her name was Ruby, and she was one of my best-kept secrets. Ruby was so shy. So delicate. Even more than the boy inside me. And I was so protective of her. I saw how girls were treated. I saw how girls were looked at. I heard how girls were talked to. We were taught that our sisters and mamas were special. All girls and women were special, and so we should treat them with respect. But people didn't practice what they taught us. They made them special, but at the same time, they were always watching them out of the corner of their eyes. When my sisters did something wrong, they were punished more than the boys were. It was like they were wrong before they did anything. When we got whippings, our sisters were beaten worse than we were. Once, Mama found some peanut butter and jelly sandwiches Sister had put in a hole in her wall. She was supposed to have been taking them for school lunches. The thumps of her body against the wall and her screams were so frightening. Daddy just went on and on beating her. We thought that he was going to kill her. I remember the sour taste of her fear. The heat of it. It made me sick in my stomach. Nobody was ever going to lay a hand on Ruby.

Inside me were mansions, and Ruby lived in them. They had clean rooms with no dirt. They had furniture that never changed places. Soft red couches. Soft blue couches. Wooden tables that soothed her when she touched them. They had kitchens where every cup and plate was perfect, in a perfect place in the cabinet. They had bedrooms with firm mattresses and soft cotton blankets and white spreads and lots of pillows. She didn't have to share her bed with anyone else. It had lots of windows, looking out at flower beds that were always in blossom, and trees, and just enough shade and just enough light. She had strawberries in her garden because she loved strawberries. Wherever she put something, it stayed there, because there was no one to come along and move it. It was always warm, and wind blew in the windows.

I was so happy when Mama and Daddy went to town and took my brothers and sisters with them. Then Ruby could come out. Many objects knew me as a girl with slender hips. She came alive for them, prancing around kitchens when no one else was home. She'd take out special teacups and saucers, plates and glasses, forks and spoons, measuring cups and bowls, whisks and spatulas—usually the same ones I insisted on using at meals. "Come on, y'all," she would say to things, with her thoughts. "Come on, everybody," and clap her hands. "They're gone, children, they're gone, honey children, they're gone, sweet friends." But she didn't talk the way you talk, with clear words. She talked with sounds, and feelings.

"You have been so good to me, red plate. Red. Red. Red. So red! Let me give you a hug! You, my favorite cup in the whole world, in the whole universe and galaxy, in all of space, in all of time, you've been so quiet today. What's wrong? Give me some water, blue glass, beautiful beautiful beautiful beautiful!" And to a tin cup, "Someone dropped you? I know. I heard the crash. I was afraid you'd be dented, but you look OK. It's OK. I'll rub you."

"Guess what I did last Sunday? I walked back from church by myself. You should have seen me. I had on this nice white dress with black shoes. And my hair was done so nicely. I cut through the woods and saw a light-green car parked over at our cousin Freda's house. I touched it with my hand because I didn't see anybody around. It was cool and hard and held my hand like water holds my feet when I step into a tub. Then I ran, trying not to get any dirt on my dress or my shoes. My shoes are so shiny! You would love them. Hey, let's turn on the radio." Then she'd pretend to dance and laugh and laugh. She'd dance and didn't care about timing or symmetry. She'd dance like she was mocking people and then stop and start laughing. After an hour or so, our family's car would pull into the driveway, and a sadness would come over her. She'd hurriedly kiss all of the things, whispering to them, and put them back in the drawers and cabinet. "Hurry, hurry," she'd say, as we heard the car doors banging and voices approaching the house. She'd look at me, smile, and disappear into my body.

Cool

One hand can't shake.

When I was around twelve, I started to realize that I had people friends who loved me. But as far as spending time together, they were friends I only had for moments at school. They weren't from Canaan's Hill. They were from the nearby town of Ashland, or from other parts of the county.

On the maps, Ashland was only three miles away, but the people who made the map didn't know what we knew. To us, Ashland was another world in another space and time. Black people in Ashland weren't as free as we were. They had yards but not fields, not woods. They lived next door to someone, and next door to someone else, and across the street from a lot of other people. They lived on the outer circles of the town, behind the center ring of white people. They couldn't have animals or gardens. Everybody around them wasn't a cousin. They weren't getting fed every day from touching the ground that echoed with their ancestors or where spirits still moved in the trees. Listening to Mama and Granny, living in town was a fall from grace.

One of my people friends was Osie Mason. When I was around fifteen, he asked me if I wanted to go to a carnival and stay overnight at his house. Doing something with someone else, or staying at somebody else's house was a new idea. We had never done anything with other kids outside Canaan's Hill. I can understand now that Osie was thinking of me as a close friend, but then I didn't realize it. It was really nice of him.

We rode on a Ferris wheel, and I closed my eyes and prayed when our seat spun upward toward the sky. I thought I would get sick. Osie's mother bought us some cotton candy, which was different from anything I had ever had. The most fun was just being in such a different place where there were so many other people. I was stunned by all of the stimulation. The dings of game machines, blinking of neon lights, and hundreds of mingling scents. The cranking of motors for the rides and the straining of ball bearings and screeching of cogs and chains made me nauseated but also drunk and giddy in a way I had never felt. I glowed like a white blaze. I dispersed into the currents.

I was amazed that night at Osie's that someone else would let me sleep in one of their beds. That they didn't seem to be guarding secrets. It was so different than in my house. Me and Osie lay awake and talked for a while as the embers of my newly found flame slowly went dim. It felt good having a friend. But the next morning I awoke feeling like a traitor, to my family and my pillows and my bed, to the secrets and shadows of our house.

Another people friend of mine was my aunt Debbie. She lived in New York City, and we were friends when she came to visit in the summer. My grandma Arlene had given birth to Mama and left her in the country with Granny so that she could go north and find a better life. It was common in those days. Later she sent for Mama, but Mama didn't want to go. Grandma remarried in New York and had seven more children, and some of them were younger than I was, like my aunt Debbie. Every summer they came to visit, sometimes all of them, sometimes only some. There was Aunt Rosie, Aunt Clara, Aunt Annette, Aunt Sandra, Aunt Debbie, Uncle Andrew, and Uncle Kenny. Those were fun times.

Everything in the country was so strange and often scary for them. They'd watch the cats eat, when we took scraps out to them and put them in a big pan, the way people watch animals in the zoo. The thick blackness of the night, without any streetlights or lights from any nearby town, was for them ominous and surreal. The snakes and the outdoor toilet. The lightning bugs spotting the darkness, and us running barefoot in grass to try to catch them, were otherworldly. The sounds of frogs croaking in the creek in the bottom, the owls, whippoorwills, cicadas, and katydids were unsettling and eerie.

My aunt Debbie sank into an open space in my heart that no one had ever touched. The things others found strange or uncool about me she simply saw and loved. We knew that we were family, but our bonding happened in an instant, like when the day is still, sunny, quiet, and then, suddenly, out of nowhere, there is a strong wind, sweeping the petals off a chrysanthemum, blowing the papers and cups from the edge of the porch, tearing the cardinal off the plum branch, and slamming the door of the barn. And then you are in motion, gathering things, holding yourself, and then there's another wind, pushing you along. After that, the day before the wind came is gone and another day has started. You don't even remember the day before. Everything has changed, the colors of things, the light, the mood. Even you are different. I was twelve, and I was taking Aunt Debbie to look at butterflies on pink gladiolas. And suddenly, the wind blew.

I rode her on the handlebars of my bicycle as often as she wanted, determined never to swerve, never to fall. I showed her secret things, a special rock, a piece of wood with a woman in the pattern of the grain, a dolphin in the knot, a hawk's feather. She went with me to feed the animals, to pull weeds in the garden. Our siblings teased us. Our parents worried and talked. But then they were leaving for New York, and I would grieve in silence and wouldn't talk, and eventually no one would think about it again, until the next summer.

My two best people friends were Malcolm and Burton, and they both lived in Ashland. We were at-school friends since first grade, but we didn't visit each other, or if we did, I don't remember it. We were brainy kids, and were from pretty strict families. We were sensitive and good in school. We spent a lot of time around older people, and it showed. We did what we were told to do and never got into trouble. We tried to get *A*'s. And we were teased by other students who were cooler than us.

We were in a boat together, sailing toward "cool." Burton was furiously paddling, and Malcolm was reading the map and giving directions. I was looking at the ripples in the water that the oars made and wondering if it was going to get chilly and if I should have brought my jacket and how fast you would have to scoop water out of the boat if it got a leak, to keep it from sinking.

The other kids were always doing something new. Clothes and hairstyles. Ways of talking or walking. Before around eleven years old, I was pretty oblivious to it all. The things I kept up with were people's colors and smells, with how they moved and how they tasted. They made fun of me sometimes, but not all of the time. I was one of them, but not really, which was all right. The teachers loved me, and that was more important.

Cool slowly crept up on us. It followed us like shadows. At first, the shadows were so far in the distance that we mistook them for some-body else's. They started to haunt us in seventh grade, and by eighth grade our shadows began to touch us, ever so gently. Our voices deepened. Burton's the most. Malcolm's a little less. Mine the least of all. We started trying out cooler ways to say things, mostly into-nations we had heard from older boys and men. We started trying out and playing with phrases. Seeing how they fit us. I was tasting phrases and seeing which parts tasted good. Of the three of us, Burton knew the most and cared the most about it. He cared the most about what others thought. Now and then I looked at how I looked in the mirror, partly because I thought mirrors were fun and looking in them made me laugh. But Burton looked at himself a lot more, without laughing. And Malcolm was still a little shy of mirrors, of looking back at himself.

I found my cool in spaces around me that others pushed aside, like finding something I loved in a dumpster. Cool was a way of decorating the distance between me and other people. I learned young that most black people would never think I was cool. I didn't know how to put it on right. To style out of someone else's style.

There was a stone inside me, in the place where you follow other people and do what they do, in the place where you understand them. It blocked the paths. If people were going right, the stone turned me left. If others were singing, it made me quiet. If people were wearing blue, it made me put on purple. And anyway, I loved flowers more than clothes. I wrote poetry. A few times I gave poems to girls, because once I was outside the friend box, in the "liking" box, I didn't know how to talk to them. Sometimes the girls looked at me like I was from some distant planet. Sometimes they didn't look at me at all. Sometimes they laughed at me with their friends. Malcolm explained it to me like this: Black life is so hard and so precarious. People are thinking about food and clothes. And here you are with your poems.

My cool came to me sometimes through tricking. I loved tricking because it made me laugh. It broke the neurologically typical world apart and made it stop and look confused. They cared so much for things being according to their words and their rules. Everything was this or that. I got good at practical jokes and tried to see if I could make certain expressions appear on people's faces. Just like a painter. I didn't think about their feelings. I moved things, so when someone came back, they looked confused. So they would see for a minute how I felt all the time. Other times, I would startle people by telling them truths they couldn't see, like a spirit was standing beside them.

My cool came in Daddy showing me how to tilt my hat to the side, to never give away my feelings. To walk like I didn't care. That wasn't so hard, because a lot of times I didn't. Cool came in the air that surrounded Uncle Charles when he occasionally came to visit. He was a ladies' man, in a Cadillac, who never let dirt touch his shoes. Every stitch of his shirts and pants was immaculate. Bright. Every color was testifying and taking a stand. But those were nothing compared to his smile and his smooth, silky voice. When he smiled the world laughed like a jazz horn. So much playfulness and light-ness. So much pure pleasure. When he spoke, the wind that had passed turned sweet and came back and passed again.

Cool came mainly in the shape of music. In the surreal bubbles of radio and television. In the snail-paced awareness of girls. Cool came as the world became smaller, more littered, like a room filling up with more and more furniture. There was less space to walk around in. Less space to think in. Less space. Less space.

By now, along with the radio, we had a telephone and a television. So, our house wasn't as quiet.

We didn't used to have a telephone. The only one for the whole community was at Granny's house. If somebody called on the phone, Granny would come out on her porch and ring a big bell and yell out the name of whomever the phone call was for in a high-pitched voice, like she was singing: "Jeeeaaan!" "Douuggglasss!" But Granny's phone didn't ring much until we started having friends in school. Then, it started ringing a lot, and that's when we finally had to get our own.

Before the television and telephone, I heard only the voices of my sisters and brothers, of Granny and Mama and sometimes Daddy filling spaces in the house. And then there were long gaps when nobody was talking or when I could hear just one faint voice somewhere outside or inside, and quiet rushed in like tides. The more things we got, the less I could hear the tides. Our house became "nicer," with better pressure from the pump for running water, with magazines, our own telephone, a bathroom with a tub. Before then, we used to take baths in a galvanized cow's tub filled with warm water in the middle of the kitchen. As the house changed and there was more noise, I got more headaches and nausea. I wandered outside more often to get away from the sounds, in search of cool air to make my headaches disappear, and to hear nothing.

I liked floating in the bubble of the radio, as long as it was turned down low. I was excited by the spirit of popular music, by its newness, its rebellion. I loved its sense of not belonging, its hunger for a new world. I knew I didn't belong in the old world. There was no place for a black boy who loved spirits more than soul, who didn't love Jesus, who was the ambassador of the plants. I was feeling Booker T's organ and Junior Walker's saxophone like the light of gold in my body. I was feeling the haunting of Bob Dylan and the engine of Jimi Hendrix's spaceship. I was feeling the wind through Joni Mitchell's flute, where seven blue moons shone full over blue waters. "It's your turn to wash the dishes," Mama's voice interjected, disrupting my rapture, or "You need to take that trash outside," or "I need you to go down to Granny's and get me a jar of tomatoes." But I was attached to the music by threads from my body. I was already tasting and dreaming of other worlds. I now knew that I had friends I hadn't met yet. I would meet them after a while.

I wanted to meet hippie friends, playing in strawberry fields with others like me, in patched jeans and bandanas. I wanted to meet friends in other tribes, like the pictures I saw and the people I read about in the *National Geographic* magazines that Mama brought home. I loved *National Geographic* magazines! I read about groups in places like China, Australia, Argentina, Tibet, Thailand, New Zealand, Kenya, Nigeria, Spain, Samoa, and Polynesia. I felt connected to them, and they all felt strangely familiar, as if I had once been one of them. I let their spirits rise from the pages and touch me and tell me things. I spent hours laughing with them.

A professor at Randolph-Macon College, in Ashland, gave the magazines to Mama. He was one of the white people she was cleaning houses for. But it caused a lot of problems in our house, because one day the professor gave Mama a ride home after work. Even though the professor was old, Daddy got the maddest I ever saw him. We could hear him yelling outside their bedroom door. "No white man is going to give a wife of mine a ride. I don't care who he is," Daddy yelled.

The story goes that when Daddy was a boy, his mama was with a white man on the plantation, and then when his daddy found out he went crazy. His daddy was working in the dairy, and his mama was working in the big house. On a day when the sky was blue with white clouds, some white men came and got Daddy's daddy and took him to a sanitarium. People from the field and the house stopped working to watch, and after that day, Daddy never saw his daddy again.

Even now, when I see a *National Geographic*, I think about Daddy's mama and his daddy, my grandma and grandpa. I think about big metal containers in the old dairy, filled with fresh milk and cream.

There was something wrong with the television. It was a gray, hungry space. It ate and ate and never got full. It stared at me like a hungry wild dog. So we fed things into it. We gave it pieces of our hearts and livers. We gave it pieces of our brains, and we fed it the most sacred thing of all—our attentions.

And the television didn't fit anywhere, with any other things. The shape of its corners and the textures of the glass screen were wrong next to anything. Next to wooden chairs or a table. Next to the couch. It pretended to be a mirror when it was turned off, but it wasn't. Mirrors are still and lively, but the television was never still.

The things I liked most about the television were the pretty wires and tubes I could see inside of it, looking through the holes in the back. The tubes lit up like lights on a Christmas tree, except they hummed, and there was an odor like something burning. I looked forward to when our televisions or radios broke, so I could take out the wires and play with them. If there were any spirits in a television, this must be where they lived. There was always a thick piece of heavy, silver metal, like a magnet, with copper wires wrapped around it. I knew this was the heart.

I knew it was the heart because it pulsed in my hand. And because I saw Daddy operating on engines all the time. When Daddy opened an engine up, he talked to all of the parts. Sometimes he talked to them gently, but other times he scolded them. Daddy never cursed, but he would say "Daggone it!" I didn't hear anyone curse until I got to college. Daddy could take any engine apart or build engines from scraps. He made table saws and engines with whetstones to file tools and engines for other things. Daddy was trained as an engineer in the army and they taught him a lot about engines, although he had already taught himself a lot before he went in. But Daddy was mad at the army because, although they trained him, they wouldn't give him the title or the engineer job. They didn't give black men much of anything when Daddy was in the army. When I took an old television apart, I could follow the trails of coiled copper and colored wires into a land of spirits who were always on edge. I could see some of where Daddy lived.

We saw a lot of people being cool on television, especially on the music shows, like *Soul Train* or *American Bandstand*. When I saw James Brown's hair on television it reminded me of my sisters. Once, when Mama was straightening Sister's hair, a scent found me that I had been hiding from. It was a foreign scent, from another world. It had tried to get me when I went to feed the chickens. It got in the corn. But I ran and washed my hands and didn't go back into the yard. I sat in the kitchen when Mama made dinner so it couldn't get past the onions and greens, or the nutmeg and cinnamon in the corn pudding. Past the biscuits, or the damson jam. Past the chicken and gravy.

I loved the kitchen more than any other room. I was always there when Mama was cooking. When I was a little boy, she couldn't take a step in the kitchen, she says, without me holding on. Mooing like a cow and holding on. The kitchen was like the church of my mama's love. Sometimes she sang gospels while she clattered pans. I walked in my mama's sighs. I feasted on her longings. In the corn bread and greens. In the apple jelly. The plum jam and ham hocks. In the biscuits and the waffles and the bacon. In fried berries and fried chicken and fried corn and fried pork chops and gravy. Her hopes were a tear soaked into a biscuit. Her dreams were a sweetness at the same time in the molasses and sorghum, in the maple syrup on top of melted butter on the other half of the same biscuit. There was always something pushing and always something pushing back. The tension between these was a cool pool of water on a sticky hot day I dove into and floated, and sank slowly down, then rose, then sank again and could not get enough. The in-between of candied yams and Virginia salt-smoked ham, of salty grits and sugar, of fried chicken and watermelon, was where my mama threw her arms open and ran ecstatically into her own rapture.

Staying in the kitchen that night worked, until after dinner. Until all the food was eaten and put away, the crumbs swept up, and the scents of dinner gone. The foreign scent that was after me couldn't break through. But later, Sister sat in a chair in the kitchen while Mama ran the hot iron along a handful of her hair, dabbing grease on her scalp. I thought the smell of hair grease and hair on fire would be thick enough to keep the other scent at bay. That, and the faint odor of leftover chicken lard. Sister screamed every so often, when the hot iron brushed against the soft back of her neck. The alien scent snuck in and settled on me like fog over the creek in the bottom. It came through the floorboards, from under the house, through the worn, yellowed linoleum.

There was a moment as long as a day when I felt it coming. And then I was down, thrashing on the floor like a hog with its throat cut, eyes rolled back in my head. I was trapped inside while the flesh was ripping away from the bones. I was splitting into a million pieces. I was drenched, underwater. There was a terrible taste of metal in my mouth, as a spoon was shoved in to keep me from swallowing my tongue. There was a long time of nothing, and then finally Mama's voice, "Red, Red, Red . . ." And I was coming back, drifting back. The light bulb in the ceiling was dimmed by Mama's head. Oh no, I thought, when I could think, it happened again. Even when I could get up, I didn't want to. But Lightnin' Hopkins's spirit came to the rescue. He played a blue note, and I followed the note with my ears as it drifted across the room, like a full moon across a midnight sky. "Get on up from there, boy!" he said in his playful, deep voice. And his gold tooth shone on me until I finally forgot my embarrassment and smiled.

James Brown's hair reminded me of my convulsions. We saw him on *American Bandstand*, sandwiched between Petula Clark and a teenager rating a new song. She gave it a ten because it had a good beat. I liked watching James Brown. After seeing him, I listened more closely to his music when it came on the radio. Something about his hair helped to heal the shame of my convulsions. It was women's hair, which seemed strange, since his songs and his performances were a lot about being a man. I wondered the same thing about him that I did about a lot of the bands and singers we saw on television and heard on the radio. I wondered if they really took themselves seriously, or if they were having fun joking. The Monkees were having fun. They were like grown kids on their television show. A playfulness also infused the music of a lot of other bands, like the Beatles. But James Brown. He just might shoot somebody as dead as Stagolee shot Billy, if they touched his hair.

The White Castle

Don't bite off more than you can chew.

Inside the white castle, I was blue, blue, blue. I was blue about every day. But I was free at last, free at last, too. I was chasing rabbits and sitting on the dock of the bay. I was chain-chain-chained, and I was looking for strawberry fields and grazing in the grass and trying to catch the wind.

Just before going to the white castle, I was in another kind of blue. Light blue like the sky. I was in blue watching television and seeing bad white people shooting the good people who stood up for our rights. They were battering peaceful black people with sticks and throwing rocks at them. They were beating them with fists and pinning them against walls and sidewalks with water hoses. They were spitting on them and yelling at them and turning dogs loose on them. I was in blue and getting bruises and aches from watching black people with their heads cracked open and their faces bloody.

I was in blue as we sat almost motionless, huddled on the couch as a black hearse passed slowly with President Kennedy's casket inside. We saw a lot of caskets on television. We saw Malcolm X's casket. And Robert Kennedy's. We saw hundreds of caskets of boys coming home from Vietnam, and caskets of student protesters shot by soldiers, and caskets of murdered civil rights workers. I wondered what it felt like to be in a casket.

I was watching Mama and Daddy's faces on the verge of tears. Black people were rioting in a lot of cities. Civil rights workers were marching all over. I heard the word "freedom" a lot, and I fell in love with it. But black people weren't the only ones who wanted freedom. Freedom! Freedom! Freedom! "Freedom," Richie Havens sang on a stage at Woodstock. There was free love in San Francisco.

White women were taking their bras off and burning them in barn fires. White students were getting shot protesting the Vietnam War. Monks in orange robes wanted freedom, as planes were dropping napalm on women and children and they were burning like torches in the fields. They set their beautiful robes on fire in protest and burned like lynched slaves. I was crying as we watched, as if we were on a boat, watching a city burn, and our boat was about to pull into that city's harbor.

I had been in blue all of my life, listening to people on Canaan's Hill talk about white people. For me and my siblings, white people had been a presence without faces. We knew them as the slave owners and their descendants. We knew them as the rulers and definers whose world our parents, grandparents, and great-grandparents entered to work in but fled as quickly as possible at the close of day. We had heard that they could be so nice when it was daytime, when it was just them, alone, talking to a black person. But they could turn mean after five o'clock, when their families came home. After dark, they could be predatory. We only saw them from a distance, the women who paid our mamas and grandmamas for housecleaning, ironing, laundry, and taking care of children. The storeowners and people who worked in stores. The policemen. The farmers. The mechanics. The insurance men. The families sitting in their nicely shaved yards.

I was in blue listening to the stories of how white men on the plantation were always after black women. How my family had to run or hide or fight back. How they were beaten and prayed for freedom. I was in blue listening to stories about how white people's houses stank and how they were a race of dirty people. Funny tales about white people were often the evening's entertainment, as Mama and Granny took turns, and we laughed until our bellies hurt. I could feel white people's hatred for us written like tattoos across the most private parts of our bodies. It bent the two races toward each other like trees arching across a roadway, filled with the sap of loathing, but also raging with hunger.

Not all white people hated us, but who did and who didn't? Some of them seemed to pity us instead of pitying themselves. Some of them were full of small courtesies. Some of them gave Mama and Granny old clothes or books. Sometimes when an older white woman was giving Mama something, she would keep holding the thing she was giving, even after it was in Mama's hands. As if she didn't really want to let go of it. And even though they gave us stuff, they never gave us anything they would really miss.

We had heard about white people who were different, who were decent. Who were ashamed of what white people had done to black people and tried to change things. Some of them were marching on television. But only a few of the different kind of white people seemed to be around where we lived. Mama sometimes worked for people like that. But they weren't brave. They wouldn't let other people know how they felt.

I was thinking about all of this when I was riding the bus way "up the country" to get to Patrick Henry, around curves on Route 54 and past fields and cows grazing. I liked watching the green and cows go by. I was thinking about how what people say about other people is one world. A half-real one at best. And I was thinking about how when you meet them, the people you've heard stories about are another world, a realer one. In the stories, there are no scents, tastes, temperatures or colors. But in the flesh, those things are overwhelmingly real. When I was riding the bus, I was curious about how, this time, the two worlds would measure up against each other.

When I first got to the white castle, I was sad. I was sad because I was hardly ever around black students. I was in all college preparatory classes, with all "smart" students who were almost all white. What happened to all of the black kids, especially the ones I thought were smarter than me. I thought that all of my friends at Gandy were smarter than me, as far as schoolwork went. I got *A*'s because I could "see" things. I dreamed a lot of my papers. It was the same way with poetry. I had to remind myself again and again that what I dreamt was really mine, that I could use it and put my name on it.

It felt a little like stealing, like cheating, because it came so easily, as if some invisible friends were passing me notes with all the answers. But my friends could do things with numbers and letters that I never could. And being smart in school was about the tricks you could do with letters and numbers.

And what happened to all the black teachers? I didn't understand then that I would never be around many black students or teachers again. For the rest of my life. I didn't realize that the world I was accustomed to was gone forever. How could a whole world disappear, just like that?

Right before integration, I had finally started learning to talk to black people, to have friends. And now I had to learn white talk. White people used different words and expressions. They wore different lines and makeup on their faces. They looked at different places on my body and let their tongues and teeth show more. They seemed to focus on a face an inch in front of the face they were talking to. They wore smiles like peace offerings. Sometimes it was really friendliness and innocence. But sometimes it was "I don't want you to see the real me. Please just disappear." It was hard for me to tell which was which. Most black people didn't trust any white people's smiles. They knew something I didn't. For many, the only world was the one in the stories they had heard. They had been shaped by them. They knew what was what in the world. They knew what was possible and what was not. But it was good in some ways that I didn't know those things. In that way, I was more ready for the new world.

I was happy in the white castle when I could escape during recess or lunch and sit behind one of the buildings facing green fields and listen to the birds and watch the cows grazing. I could hear the pattern of sounds the students and teachers made, coming and going from one building to another, milling around inside classrooms. Their talking was like the leaves of prairie grass and alfalfa blowing in the wind. I could close my eyes and see their colors. A patch of intense green clustered around the doors to the cafeteria. A patch of red hovering like a cloud near the gym.

But I was sad, sitting in back of the school or in classrooms, when I thought about the pictures of black children standing outside white schools, while white mobs threw bricks and other things at them. The mobs were like rabid dogs, frothing at the mouths, barely held back by policemen. So, that's where we stood. Black people said it was what we had to do. It was for a good cause. But I imagined those children's terror. I felt some of it. I thought it was cruel to send them there. There were no protests when we went to the white castle, but we were so alone. There was no one to talk to because no one else had been through it. All the things that people said were from an older world, but we were in another world now. And no one knew what things to say for the new world.

In some ways, I was feeling more at home in the white castle than I had at my other school. No one made fun of me. No one assumed anything. I liked that there was more space in which to move. I liked the newness. I was happy that we had to stand farther away from each other and really look. I liked the distance. I liked that there were so many more possibilities for how conversations could go, for what we could talk about.

I liked being given a blank canvas so I could paint any picture I wanted to. I was feeling good and clean, learning and reading and listening to interesting discussions and ideas. For the first time, I felt that some people saw me as just me. They were not my kin and they knew nothing about my family. All they had was right in front of them—a delicate, black cyborg, a bright, soft-edged Frankenstein, a quiet splotch of rhythmic sound and color. I liked the freedom of the white castle. I liked it so much that I broke the rules I had been given at home. There was a rule that said, "Never tell white people your secrets." But I liked some of the people I met there so much, I broke the rule to pieces.

Most of my friends were girls. I was enjoying having conversations with them, learning about new things and different ways of seeing the world. Talking about Van Gogh and Emily Dickinson. Talking about the nature of the universe. Sharing albums like Joni Mitchell's *Blue* and books like *Jonathan Livingston Seagull*, *The Little*

Prince, The Rubaiyat, On Walden Pond, The Black Poets, The Collect-ed Poems of Emily Dickinson, The Bell Jar, Ecclesiastes, The Song of Solomon, The Family of Man, and *The Prophet.*

My friends told me things and showed me things. A lot of them were gay, or lesbian, or bisexual, but nobody used those words back then. People just said, "Oh, he's 'funny'" or "You know, she's 'different.'" No one had a language for coming out yet.

One of my best friends I ever had was white, and like with a lot of my friends, her parents didn't want her talking to black kids. So we had to be secret friends. Her name was Janie, and she used to worry a lot about me. She used to say, "You're like the Princess and the Pea." I didn't know who the princess was or why she had a pea, but I understood that Janie meant I was sensitive, and that everything affected me too much.

I learned all the paths through the white castle. Sidewalks and hallways and cut-across grass. But I couldn't get the hang of the social paths. My head was spinning, but I refused to let anybody know it. The biggest thing was that I was somebody instead of nobody. I was very popular and well-liked. I was even admired. But why? I liked being liked, but I also hated all the attention. I was feeling the "real *mes*" just crying inside.

I was being asked to join so many things, like the Beta Club, Key Club, The National Honor Society, and Spanish Club. The thing was, I had no idea what any of them were. I liked the sound of them, and I understood they were honors. When I was a junior, I was asked to run for student government president. But I had never heard of student government. I understood I was being asked to play the role of a leader, and it seemed like an important thing to do. When I thought about it, I imagined that I would have the chance to change things. I was excited that people liked me enough to ask me to run. When people asked me to do things, I often thought that it meant they could see something that I couldn't—that they could see who I really was and what I should be doing.

The other person they asked to run was a friend from my old school, Gladys Patterson. I liked Gladys. She was smart and always so poised. White students were trying to welcome us by having two black kids run for president. They were trying to say, this school belongs to all of us. But not everybody felt that way. "The devil never sleeps," my granny said when a white student protested and insisted that his name be added to the ballot. His motto was "We need to make it fair to white people." That's when things in the white castle starting falling apart. I could feel it like the drone of an approaching twister, the blue light and the clouds turning dark.

On the day of our speeches, I was shaking. I was shaking and talking to Jeremiah and Lizzy. I was shaking until I saw a group of birds flying in a low circle around a cow in a field. Then I joined them. I was in a folding chair, at the front of the gym, along with the other candidates, but I was also in the field. All of the bleachers were filled. The principal, the vice principal, and most of the teachers, coaches, and staff stood against the walls near the entry doors with serious expressions on their faces. It was rumored that students were planning to walk out in protest when the white candidate got up to give his speech. The tension was so thick that it was hard to breathe.

Everything happening was a first, so no one could play their roles because they didn't know what they were yet. I often enjoyed those kinds of moments, in spite of my anxiety. People wore emotions on their bodies in deep colors. People left their faces open. When I looked into the bleachers I could see Van Gogh-like splotches of green and blue, here and there, swirling splotches of orange and red. I could see hearts. I don't remember what I said in my speech. I don't even remember getting up to give it. I remember the applause. I remember feeling that the cheers were as much for the moment as they were for me. Students did walk out when the white candidate got up to give his speech. The slow exodus was somber as a funeral, as angry and dignified as a civil rights march.

I won the election and became the new president of the white castle. People wrote their hopes on my body. They wrote notes and tattoos on my spirit. I wanted to heal things, like my mama, Jesus, Martin Luther King, or Gandhi. Other people thought I could do it, so I thought so too.

But I was feeling too much blue. I was starting to break apart from never being alone. The weight of everything was starting to crush me. I was feeling almost all the time that I was lost in a strange land. The constant anxiety in my belly came roaring out at night, in my room at Granny's. I broke things on purpose. Precious things. I tore up some of my favorite books. I tore up *Go Up for Glory* and *On Walden Pond*. I tried to get meals from the blue of Muddy Waters's guitar. From his voice. From the blue of Joni Mitchell's album cover. From her high-pitched moaning. I was lost even among the familiar. I had wandered far into the forest, and I hadn't left behind any crumbs. I ached so badly from the isolation, but I couldn't think clearly enough to understand why I was aching. Things were moving too fast, and I was being swept along, like in white water, just trying to grab some air when I could.

I was doing too many things. I was taking piano lessons, playing for the church choir. I was teaching myself to play acoustic guitar. I was pushing myself to play basketball. I was writing poetry. I was still the *A* student and the "pet" for all of my teachers. I was a "cool" guy for my friends. I was a fun brother. I was the champion of the animals and plants. I was the echo of my mama and my granny's second sight. I was a gateway for the spirits, their friend and companion. I was getting so good at "passing" that I didn't even know anymore that I was doing it. I wanted so badly to believe I was normal.

I had moved out of my mama's house to be alone and try to find my real self. It was too noisy, and we had all gotten bigger, and the house felt too small. And I had read *Sons and Lovers*, and it scared me. I was so content around my mama that I thought that if I didn't make myself leave, I would end up living there forever. So I moved upstairs at my granny's house, where I could have a room of my own and quiet. I ate at Mama's house, used the bathroom there, watched television sometimes and hung out with my sisters and brothers, but like Granny, I retreated to the quiet.

It worried me that I had no desire, and I felt that I needed to fix that. I would go looking for desire. But I didn't know where to look. I looked in magazines. I looked in girls' faces. In the mirrors of their skin. Sometimes I would find it when I thought about the chubby boy in the locker room. Locker rooms were a big thing. It was the first time that black and white kids could legally see each other naked. There were a lot of desires in locker rooms. They were like a sea of flames, in the boy's locker room. They would sometimes spill out of the girls' locker room like a giant wave or tear drop and rush through the doorway to the boys' locker room and swallow us whole. Sometimes I would find desire when one of my sister's friends stayed over at our house, and playing, took my hand and rubbed it against her breasts. Sometimes desire would find my body when I was missing, when I was deeply asleep.

I often fell asleep and dreamed that the earth had been scorched by fire. Thousands of animals, dead, their carcasses rotting in fields and on the roads. Piles of Frigidaires and old burnt-out cars littering the streets. The air as orange as sunset all the time, copper, thick, and hard to breathe. In my dreams, we were living in a shelter of wooded overgrowth, extended by an awning made of plastic tarp and held up by poles of cut sycamore. We foraged for food. There was no more time. There was nowhere we had to go and no place we had to be. A pack of crows cawed in nearby oak trees before taking off, hurrying down the southern sky. I was as happy as I was when I was little, and Mama and Daddy and Granny and all of my sisters and brothers were at home. I was walking to get water from a nearby well and turned my head to look back, and suddenly, I was in a meadow, all alone, at dusk, and then I woke up.

And then I would lie awake the rest of the night, listening to tires singing on Interstate 95, several miles away. When the night was clear, the sounds roared through the trees like waves of a tsunami, and we were buried, like Atlantis, beneath volumes of seawater. The spirits of diesel truck engines were merciless and blindly obsessed with motion, with the demolition of stillness and reason. They were on fire with a foreign fever that frightened me. The spirits of cars were enraged, obscenely discontented. Out there, everyone had to get somewhere in a hurry. They couldn't wait. They hadn't seen us yet, because they were so self-absorbed, so delighted with the power of their noises, with their speed. But I knew that eventually they would notice us.

They would find us, and this time, they would be more careful than they had been during slavery to make sure that none of us survived. They would find the butterflies, and the moths, and the sparrows, and the thrushes. They would find the crickets in the meadows, and the blueberries, and the apples, and the cherries, and the corn. They would find the spirits in the begonias and hollyhocks, in the Sweet Williams and roses, in the sweet gum and dianthus and morning glory and peas. But I would fight for them. I would fight with everything I had, even with my body. I would be a guerilla fighter if I had to and live in the wilderness. Or I would wear disguises and fight them from the inside. I would fight them until my dying breath.

In my room at my granny's house, I was looking in the mirror and seeing a Frankenstein. I was trying to stitch myself back together at night, where I was coming apart. I was burning candles and losing myself watching the flames. I was turning on my black light and staring at my mushroom poster. I was praying to the universe. I was reading Emily Dickinson and Han Shan. I was listening to the blue of Lightnin' Hopkins and Jimi Hendrix, and Roberta Flack. I was cutting myself and bleeding on pages of a girlie magazine I had found beneath knee-deep layers of old newspapers in the old abandoned chicken coop. I looked in the mirror again, and who did I see standing behind me, smiling, but the devil, stubbled and unshaven. I hugged my pillows and whispered to Jeremiah and Lizzy and waited for the spirits of old people who once lived in Granny's house to start coming out of the walls.

I was so deep in blue that I thought I couldn't go any deeper. But as it turned out, there was no bottom to colors. As president, I had to keep doing things. I had to keep holding on to my form. There was a student government conference in a hotel in Charlottesville, Virginia, and I had to go to it.

I had never been in a hotel before. To me, it was really fancy, like something on television. There were so many big rooms, nice carpets, and chandeliers. The halls were a buzzing, spastic sea of white bodies. I was feeling lost in the whiteness, in the noise. The brightness of the lights made me dizzy. In the close crowds in the hallways and lobby, I was elbowed and shoved, and sometimes fondled. Curious eyes peered through me, like I was a window. Hostile eyes scowled at me. Soft pink lips spat "nigger," and sneers and laughter waited around every corner. A girl looked at me and licked her lips, as if I was a piece of candy. I wanted to curl up into a ball. The sounds ripped me from the banks and swept me out into cold waters. And the waters replaced my bones. The waters ate through me.

I got so dizzy I started falling, like in a dream. Jeremiah, Lizzy, and Beulah sang to me. They were holding tightly to my hands and trying their best to break my falling. Lizzy was wearing an orange dress with flowers. Jeremiah was wearing a green T-shirt. Beulah had her hair in bangs. The spirit of Emily Dickinson was holding my hand for a while, but we got separated in the crowd. I was searching for her turquoise glow in the packed corridors and lobby, but I couldn't find it. Then someone announced the results of an election in a large assembly hall, and I was devastated to hear that someone else had been elected president. I didn't understand that these were regional offices, not school ones. "I thought I was president!" I said to myself, thinking I must be the victim of a cruel joke.

I was stumbling along the hallway when a hand reached out and led me into a bedroom filled with raucous laughter. White teenagers were joking and passing around cups of rum and soda. I recognized some of them from our school. "Come on, have some," a girl with a friendly smile said and handed me a cup. Some of the others whooped, shared laughs, and ignored me. But I was watching them, nervously, as their faces turned redder the more they drank. I had heard that when white people start drinking, the redneck in them comes out. So I should never be around white people once their faces get red.

But I didn't know what I should do. So I drank some of the rum someone handed me, like Adam eating the apple. *Why not?* I was thinking. *Maybe it will stop the pain.* But I had never even smelled liquor before. It burned so much going down, it burned a path like fire burning dry grasses, and the taste gagged me, like drinking water from a pig trough. There was a moment of lightheadedness, but then came the dizziness, deep purple vertigo. I was watching Jeremiah, Lizzy, and Beulah looking at me with such concern. "Come on," Jeremiah said, pulling on my arm. "Come on. Let's go find your room." But a tiredness overcame me, and I couldn't move. A hopeless thing moved beneath my skin. I lay down and closed my eyes and listened to the crackling of fire burning all of the trees in the forest.

I was following the trail of fire when a girl's voice said, "Here, I'm giving you a squirrel." *A squirrel*, I thought, *why would I want a squirrel?* But then she patted my arm and said it again. "Don't you want it?"

I rolled onto my stomach and opened my eyes, and after a minute, I got it. Everything under a girl's skirt is some kind of animal. I had learned about beavers. Beavers had teeth and they would bite whatever came near them. Then there were furry kittens and cats. They would rub against you and purr. And now there were squirrels. Squirrels were what a thousand black men had been lynched for. But I was in the white castle world now, so what happens?

A foot away her skirt edged up, and she opened her thighs. I closed my eyes but I could still see it, the cotton, the taboo, the promise. I was still hypnotized. I would stay that way. "You didn't even look," she said, smiling, handing me another cup.

"I thought I was president! I thought I was president. I thought I was president," I said. She got me up and helped me back to my room and held me as I threw up all night, mumbling and crying out. "You are. Don't worry. You are the president," she said and rubbed my head and became my friend.

I was just trying to be the best president I could, and still live, but a lot of people were treating me like I was a priest. The old people at church were always patting my head and saying, "This boy goin' to be a preacher," but I was always saying to myself, "Over my dead body." I was finding out now that being a leader didn't suit me. Imagining was fun, but having to be talking and holding myself together all of the time was no fun at all. Inside the white castle, I heard many confessions. I heard prayers. I heard first and last rites. I heard reflections, and hopes, and regrets. I heard them from coaches, teachers, principals, vice principals, janitors, and I heard them from students. I was a blue light lighting things by listening.

I was sharing this all with the slaves who were in the fields surrounding us, among the cows and blue jays in their tattered clothes, keeping watch. When things were hard for us, the slave children walked across the pastures and moved among us. They moved their hands across our foreheads and caught our tears in the shredded, dingy burlap and cotton of their shirtsleeves and dresses. They leaned close and whispered and sang to us.

Sometimes I talked to Jeremiah about the people in the white castle. "They are nice people," I told him, "most of them. But why are they telling me their secrets?"

"You know why," he said. "Because someday you'll tell them."

But in the end, I couldn't save the white castle. I couldn't even save myself. The white castle was torn apart by what the television called a riot in the spring of 1972. It was bound to happen. Two countries were coming together, but one country wanted to rule. Black students had never sung the "Star-Spangled Banner." We sang our own anthem, "Lift every voice and sing / till earth and heaven ring / ring with the harmonies of liberty." I loved the black national anthem. It made me cry sometimes, just thinking about the journeys of black people in this strange country. But it had never crossed white people's minds that we had an anthem.

Why would we have sung the anthem of a country that wouldn't let us be a part of it? That only postponed our genocide so we could slave to make it rich? We wanted to sing both anthems at assemblies. That would have been fair. We wanted the white school to respect our culture and our history, just like we were being asked to respect theirs. But the principal kept saying there's only one country. There's only one anthem. So some of us sang our anthem at the next assembly anyway.

One thing led to another, and another thing led to the next thing, just like in a book. The principal suspended students. Other students protested the suspensions by gathering on the lawn and boycotting classes, like the sit-ins we had seen on television. I had been having such a perfect day. It was so peaceful. Sparrows were singing and flitting around the gutters. Bees flew through the schoolyard drunk with pollen. Cows grazed in the slight distance of fields. The sun was warm, and my bare arms were radiant and tingling. Slave spirits were even resting by the buildings while their children played ring games on the lawn. It was like a festival that was about to explode.

Jeremiah sat beside me in a classroom, whispering, "Don't worry. Don't worry." A minute later the gray, state trooper cars descended on the school grounds like locusts, lights blinking, and with their guns and batons, black boots and sunshades, they dragged students to buses. The heavy tastes of hate and fear overwhelmed me. The sounds of people being handled by rough white hands made my head feel like it was being battered in a boxing ring. I could taste pee, soaking jeans. I could taste the thick, salty floods from hairy sweat glands, tears, and shock. I could hear the whispers of terror like fine hairs standing on flesh. I could taste our whole past in that moment when they told us they were taking students to jail.

Parents were storming the front office. Every feeling that belonged behind bars, every thought that didn't need to be spoken, walked back and forth across the school grounds and through the office. It became a different place, a new place, with colors like in late autumn the day before the colors disappear. Television stations were getting it on camera, and the newspaper crews were writing it in their notebooks. Black parents were screaming at me, "This is all your fault!" "You're supposed to be keeping things in check!" White parents were screaming with their looks. Reporters were shoving microphones in my face. Everyone was forgetting I was still a child. I was too numb to think. I wanted to keep staring at the light on the station's camera, but before I knew anything, it was gone. I saw myself on the evening news. I was saying, "We had a good thing going." And then I was saying, "The problem is the parents. If parents would mind their own business and leave the kids alone, we could work things out. We could go forward." Then the telephone started ringing.

I watched something shattering inside the white castle, and it was so sad. The egg cracked open, prematurely, and fear rushed out. I watched it eating the magic. It was like watching a werewolf in a shadow-covered alley, nothing but a shadow himself, feeding on human flesh. And then it was gone. What could have been, but now will never be.

I watched a blue depression settle on us, like a soft rain. "Where the tree falls," my granny said, "there it must lie." What happened broke people. We came to class and wept. Some of us were getting drunk and high. Even the "good" students. It was sometimes hard for some of us to look at each other now. We didn't speak. We didn't know what to say. The old words didn't fit. And because we didn't speak, we sank deeper. A silence came. The birds stopped singing in the tall grasses behind the buildings. Cows moved farther off, into the distance. There was no one to turn to or to talk to. Lizzy and Jeremiah and Beulah could put their arms around my soul, but they couldn't cradle my body. We were in a new world our parents had never known. They didn't know what to tell us. Their helplessness was an extra weight. We had seen people shoot the good leaders, Kennedys, Martin Luther King, Malcolm X. We had seen the Black Panthers stalked and imprisoned. Was there really no standing up without being beaten down?

I was rocking back and forth on my bed. My body often stopped working and a glass I was holding would fall to the floor and shatter.

Sometimes I would just slump to the floor. One half of my face and body drooped like objects in a Dali painting. My spirit kept leaving my body, soaring and looking down at myself, soaking wet under blankets and patina sheets. I was reading Sylvia Plath's *The Bell Jar* and Emily Dickinson. I was writing a poem and then bursting into tears and then writing another poem and then bursting into tears. Granny said maybe a bad witch was riding me. She put pans of water under the bed and sprinkled salt around it. Mama prayed. And prayed, and prayed.

I was wondering why I ended up with a bad witch following me. There were plenty of good witches. But my witch didn't just ride me in my bed; she took me to her house. It was always freezing. The floor and the walls were made of cold stone. Nowhere was there any heat. She kept me in a room like a jail cell. I could dream the world my body walked in back home, but I couldn't feel it. In the daytime, I would take my shirt off and lie down on the ground, trying to rediscover the real. Trying to stop the pain moving up and down in my belly, like there was a pig trapped beneath the skin. Trying to get the world to stop spinning. Trying to catch up with where I was and what I was feeling.

One day, I just resigned myself to living in the witch's house. I hated it, but it started to be familiar. As soon as I fell asleep, she came into the cell and got on top of me. Sometimes she whipped me for hours and sank sharp teeth into my flesh. She leaned over and whispered in my ear, and I could smell the stench of her breath and the fetid odor of black gossamer and cotton. I began to stink and my ribs started poking through my skin. I didn't know anymore what was dead or what was alive. I knew I could never go back home. I knew that I would never be the same person. I knew that no matter how hard I tried, I would never get my old life back. I would have to learn to live all over again, as some other person.

The Big Yellow House

You can't have your cake and eat it too.

When I got to college, I was like a black boat floating in a white ocean, like a black bird flying in a white sky with nowhere to land. I was so disoriented. There were too many islands, and I was getting lost in the waters between them. The first year I lived at home, and each time I traveled the gray stretch of asphalt and concrete on Interstate 95 to Richmond, I lost my focus. I lost myself. I wasn't anywhere. My self was like a person in a movie whose hands and feet are tied to four horses, and the dictator gives the signal, and the soldier slaps the horses, and they bolt in different directions, and just keep on running. I knew the islands in the black sea. Granny's and Mama's houses, and the church down the road and through the woods, where I played the piano for the junior choir and taught Sunday school. But I had to learn the islands in the white sea. This building and that building. This department and that department.

I was feeling so overwhelmed and desperate. I didn't even really know what college was. What were the rules? There was a cobblestone alley near the main campus plaza, and I would go there a lot to get away from the rivers of people rushing all around me. The alley was full of old spirits and shadows that danced like reeds in the wind. It was filled with separate paths. Each path went up and down differently, had a different temperature, a different wind, and made different music when I stepped on it. I closed my eyes and tried to walk from one end of the alley to the other without changing paths. I could hear the echoes of my footsteps vibrating between the buildings on either side. I was sitting in the alley one day, holding my hand a fraction of an inch away from the sunshine and wondering, *How did I get here? What is this place?* No one had told me anything about college. Mama and Daddy didn't know anything to tell me.

I would look out from the alley, or the top window of a building, and see all the people going places and doing things. They were going to classes and to the library. They were going to restaurants and parties and meetings and clubs. They were going home and coming back and going home again. They were throwing Frisbees and catching buses and riding bicycles. There were tides of talking and laughter, of heels on sidewalks and asphalt. I was seeing them like Frankenstein peeping around a corner.

What I really wanted to do when I got out of high school was go and live on a commune. That was more where my heart was, but I was afraid of letting go of everything I knew. Guest speakers had come to our high school for a cultural program, and they told us all about their commune. It sounded like such a peaceful place. I wanted to get out of the hard things, like concrete, or classrooms with headaches. I wanted to lie in grass and gaze up for hours at the clouds. But I was used to doing the safest things, the things I was supposed to do. I was black, *and* I was "different." And so I came here, even though I couldn't remember coming.

When I got to college, I still hadn't recovered from high school. I hadn't had time to heal. I was so tired of having glass things slip from my fingers and fall and break. Of spiraling downward all night. Of cold sweats and weakness in my body that seemed to deepen. Of feeling doomed. So I secretly decided to leave, to go somewhere else. Anywhere. To try and find something to keep me going. I didn't realize yet that there was nowhere else to go.

At first I planned to ride a freight train, like the men in blues, but I couldn't find the train. So, I hitchhiked to Chapel Hill, North Carolina, because I had met someone who lived there and the words were in my mind. A black man picked me up going out of Richmond and dropped me in South Hill, Virginia. Another older black man picked me up there and took me to Chapel Hill. It was like the men were angels who were waiting for me. The last angel looked at me like a deacon in church and said, "You be careful now, young man" as he put me out. I hummed one of my granny's spirituals, and I watched for a long time as his car disappeared. It was only after he had gone that I realized I had nothing to eat, no money, and nowhere to go. I was so hungry that I thought I would fall and not be able to get up. I was feeling like someone had scooped out some of my insides.

In an abandoned field not far from a gas station, I sat down under darkening skies and prayed that no policemen would see me. But what was I going to do? Where was I going to go? Where was there to go? I would never be free in America. I was black. I was slow in a world that was getting faster. I was soft in a world that was getting harder.

I thought about the girl in the movie *Carrie*. She was like me. When I saw the movie I cried for two weeks. I didn't talk for seven more days. It was worse when I saw *The Elephant Man*. I almost had another nervous breakdown. I remember thinking that being black and slow in America was like being a caveman in a land of dinosaurs. Always hunted. Always hyper alert.

I started walking, looking for a bright spot. A color that would touch me in the right place and make me feel better. A shape that would steady the spinning. Something I could taste that would turn all of the bitterness sweeter. And then I saw it. It shone out of the darkness like a star. Like a window with the sunshine and the bright-blue sky on the other side of it. A big yellow house on a hill in the distance, surrounded by blue-black darkness, by a night sprinkled with little lights and occasional headlights winding around curved streets. The motion-detector lights had come on in the front of the house, and there was a silver-blue car in the driveway. The yellow smiled at me, like the answer to a prayer. The yellow of canaries. The yellow of spring jonquils. The yellow of saffron. The yellow that vibrates in waves of light, that is never completely still, and so it makes stillness out of whatever is around it. Yellow framed by white trim, and that framed by deep-green grasses and trees. I imagined what it might be like living in the big yellow house, having a "normal" life. Having parents who could take care of me and protect me. Having friends and the warmth of a happy family.

For a long time I stood there, smiling back at the big yellow house. Feeling better. Breathing. And then I found another field and huddled in my sleeping bag and wept. I wept as I had been weeping almost every day since high school. I wept for my friends who had passed away. I wept for warmth I longed for but didn't have. I wept because I hadn't escaped. The witch had found me. I could hear her laughing and rubbing her hands together, like a woman's legs rubbing against a skirt. I could hear dogs barking in the distance and cars and truck tires whining on the highway. I could hear Muddy Waters's spirit in the voices of frogs, in the distant rumbling of an airplane. It blanketed me like a fog. Through the fog I saw Jeremiah's eyes as big as the sky, filled with stars, and gazing into them, I fell deeply asleep.

I don't remember how I got back. But then I was lying in bed at my family's house. I don't know what happened in between being in the field and being in the bed. Daddy was looking down at me and crying. He hugged me for the first time since I was about seven years old. "Don't you want to live in the world?" Daddy asked me.

"No, sir," I said. "I'm sorry, Daddy, but I don't. I want the world to live in me, beside the other worlds. But don't worry, I'll be all right." There were tears and deep sighs in his breathing, and I could tell by the way he held me that he didn't think I would survive. I could tell he wanted to make sure he hugged me in case he never got another chance.

After that, I would keep looking for my yellow house. I had no idea how I would ever find it, but I knew I had to. The yellow house would be safety. It would be filled with love and goodness. Once I got inside the yellow house, I would seldom have to come out. It would have staircases and a pantry like the one at my granny's. It would have big windows that let in lots of light.

I had a girlfriend the last year of college, but she didn't live in a yellow house. She was white, and her building was red brick. It was not the red of flower blossoms, though, and so I hesitated to go in there. I had to make it a yellow house in my mind. I had to paint it. Some nights I stayed at her house, in the "capital of the Confederacy," with all the white people with Confederate flags and tattoos filling the city around us.

Inside her house, with her and her two roommates, was like being in a family. Sometimes her sister came over and we had meals together and talked about the day. But in the morning, I was running home to my attic apartment as fast as I could, after looking outside to see if any Ku Klux Klan members had been watching. When I got halfway home in the stillness of pre-sun, the spirits of the city would start to dance with me. They would come out of the cobblestones and grates, gutter downspouts, bricks and stones. They would come out of alleys.

There was the spirit of an older black man with a horse and wagon in one alley. He was from before there were streets. He would take an apple from a branch and feed it to his horse, patting him on the head. Watching him made me feel less lonely. It was like watching the black janitors and servers at events I went to, like receptions and conferences. When I went to those things, I always moved toward the black "help." I could talk to them and feel more human. They were always the most beautiful and interesting people in the rooms. Watching a woman or a man holding a tray and looking so out of place was like looking at pictures of myself.

So, I was walking to my girlfriend's house one night. Walking up Monument Avenue, in the shadows of all the giant metal statues of Confederate generals on their horses. I was holding the moon in my left hand and the North Star in my right hand when a pickup truck passed and a shower of beer bottles crashed around me, one of them shattering against the side of my head. The shouts of "nigger" and loud laughter crashed into me like stones and continued to echo, mixing with the roars of the truck's engine as it careened off down the street. I froze. And then I shook. I shook like I was coming apart. I tried to cover myself with darkness, the way Adam and Eve tried to cover themselves with leaves.

When I could finally move, I tried to pick my humiliation out of the pieces of broken glass on the sidewalk. I got down on my knees, cutting them, cutting my fingers, trying to clean the glass up, to undo it all. I heaved. I tried to tear the rage out of the streetlights. I wanted to kill the men in the truck. I wanted to annihilate any memory of them ever having existed. I went home to my room and tore my clothes off. I cried. I showered. I sobbed until my body didn't belong to me. I lay awake into the next morning.

By the time I was getting used to things in college, it was over. Then I was lost. I had gotten used to a routine, to the buildings and streets. I knew every angle of the houses on the streets. I knew every step and every crack in the sidewalks. I knew every shrub, every tree, and every angle and patch of sky through branches in all of the seasons and every spirit that lived beneath them. I knew the decibel of sound on every street, alley, foyer, hallway, stairway, auditorium, and classroom. I knew the birds and their songs. I knew where they built their nests. I knew the scents of every place. I didn't know the colors of all of the cars or buses or trucks and when they passed, but I knew the surges of their sounds, the waves, the ebbs and the tides.

But now the streets all turned blue, glowing like luminescent waves of seawater in the dark. I was afraid to walk on them, but I had to. And when I did, my mind was swept away. I would stand for an hour in one place, or try to find a familiar chair in a familiar place and just sit there. Overnight, everyone had disappeared. They had abandoned me. The city had already forgotten me, and I hadn't even left yet. The charcoal-colored rooftops. The tin grates and vents and air ducts. The tall brick chimneys. The cobblestones of Monument Avenue. They wouldn't look at me. They wouldn't talk to me. And then the blossoms were coming. The dogwoods were coughing blood and laughing. The cherry blossoms were floating my arms up to the sky, like wings, but I didn't want to fly. I fought to stay grounded. The magnolias dripped their syrup into my dreams, and when the wind blew, the fleshy petals curled around my naked chest and I became nothing but scent. There was a shroud around me, a thin gown that scrambled patterns and distorted things. The music of the cars and trucks became metal noise. The birds were like randomly dripping faucets at midnight. People's voices were all shouts, commands, and arguments. Sunlight burned me like it had when I was a child.

I had gone to college like I was supposed to. But what happened now? Where did I go now? Where could I find joy? I didn't understand the process for finding a job, and I didn't really want one. I knew I couldn't work nine to five; I couldn't hold up. I would flop over like a canvas sack. I would end up banging my head against things or cutting my thighs. I needed bright spots in my mind. I needed good things to think about; otherwise, I would get deeper and deeper into the forest, just standing in one place. Anxiety and shame would eat me up from the inside, like giant tapeworms. I would become nothing more than a host. I needed good things to think about to have good feelings. Without good feelings, I would not survive.

My new girlfriend, Virginia, was a bright spot. I had just broken up with my old girlfriend because I didn't know what else to do. We talked about marriage, but she didn't want to marry me. Marrying out of your race back then was like going up against the world. I couldn't have survived it. The world wasn't just outside; it was inside too. In rooms. In furniture. In scents. In our heads. When I thought about what we would do next, nothing came up.

The word "Virginia" was hibiscus. It was a blue lake and a blue sky and a blue robin's egg. It was the bright spot I had been looking for. So I started writing her poems and love letters, and we started holding each other quietly in the evenings. Virginia was going to California to do an internship, so I said to her, "Why don't I come? Why don't we just move there together? Why don't we find a yellow house?" And like that, the decision was made.

When I told my family that I was moving to California, no one believed I would really go. I was the one they thought would never leave home. They thought I would never leave because I needed to be taken care of. But I was rebelling against being taken care of. I wanted to show them that I could take care of myself. I wanted to be free, to get out of my daddy's shadow, and get outside my mama's second sight. I wanted to have a direction, so I could move instead of just standing or sitting in one place or hiding in secret places the way I had been doing. I wanted to see new places and things.

From the Greyhound bus window, I saw stretches of yellow, brown, and green that lasted for hours. But I didn't see much red or pink, or blue or indigo. The bus stank and the people on it were strange. I listened closely to them talking to each other, and I lay my head against the window most of the time, because it was cool, like a washcloth.

Sometimes the bus pulled off the freeways and wove around abandoned and haunted streets with wide splotches of grease and oil, dried blood and vomit. There were often boarded-up buildings with broken faces and nearby fields with pieces of car metal, glass, old couches, and tin cans. When we pulled into the stations, I never wanted to get off, but sometimes we had to, because we had to change drivers and buses. I worried about them losing my suitcase. I worried about leaving something on the bus. I worried about leaving something in a bathroom or on a seat in the station. I clutched my things to me like a bag lady, hunching over so that my chin could help to hold them. Outside the doors of the station were often pimps looking for tender and frightened bodies. They were like the witches in fairy tales, giving candy to children. In the bathrooms there were often men who tried to take my things or sweet talk me into giving them blowjobs, or when that failed, to wrestle me into stalls.

After three days, the bus reached water, and me and Virginia couldn't stop hugging. We moved into a big yellow building on the Duboce Triangle, right near Market and Castro Streets. Living together looked like it should be easy, but a lot of times it wasn't. There was so much going on all the time outside the window, and I wanted to explore everything, to taste everything. And then, being around someone else all of the time was hard. I couldn't let go and dissolve. Studies say people with ASD have trouble with romantic relationships. The studies say that some of us can't love, but from what I've seen, the people who can't love aren't autistic. I have been fortunate to love, and be in love, and to have relationships. Virginia and me bonded and loved the way outcasts do, when all they have is each other. But I kept having trouble being a stable partner, being the man. I saw men partners on television and in movies, on the streets or in restaurants. They were so at ease. They knew how the world worked. But I could never get the hang of it. I could be a good friend. I could be the best of friends. But the rules of friendship are green. And the rules of relationship are purple.

Me and Virginia were together for seven years. Some of it was stormy, and some of it was calm. But I was the storm maker, the twister, the hurricane. When I was with Virginia, I wanted to have everything, but I didn't know that that's not the way life is. I wasn't good at sharing some of my most personal thoughts or feelings, partly because I seldom knew what they were. It would not have crossed my mind to share about my friendships with spirits. And the regular things, like what I did in school or whom I talked to or what they said were forgotten by the end of the day. I wanted to do everything I could imagine doing. I didn't know that it wasn't possible. I wanted to meet everybody, as long as they couldn't see me. I wanted to study love and sex and take notes in my body. I wanted to see how different scents turned me into different people. I wanted to keep going on my adventure. Virginia wanted the things that are considered normal, but I couldn't give them to her.

And then there was the race thing we never talked about. It never seemed to come up. And so, even if I had been "normal," I don't know how things would have worked. Our first Christmas in California, we flew home to visit our families. We planned to stay for a few days at her family's house in Northern Virginia and then for a few days at my family's house on the plantation. But when we got to her family's house, they wouldn't let me in. They didn't want her going out with a black person. It was cold outside, not just from the weather. Her brother had to take us in. I don't have words for how bad I felt. Sometimes I don't cry when things happen, not until a long time afterward, because it takes a while for anything to sink in. And most of the time, so many other things come up before the first thing sinks in that when I do cry, I'm not sure which thing I'm crying about. I didn't cry about that night for a long time. By the time I cried about it, I was in another yellow house, with another girlfriend, and we were about to move.

The Purple Time

*Religion is a dream the body
sends the mind.*

In the purple time, I forgot the things they say you always have to remember; at least, I forgot them with my mind. I forgot that I was a man. I forgot that I was black. I forgot that I came from a plantation in the South and that I was close to my family. I forgot about my family. I forgot to call or write. I forgot that I had gone to graduate school and gotten an MA and a PhD, and I forgot that I was supposed to have ambition and be doing things in the world. I forgot that I was a poor person, an inch away from the streets. And I remembered things I had been forgetting most of my life. I remembered what made me happy. I remembered how hard it was, in the world, and that it had never been my world in the first place. I remembered how to let go, and laugh, and smile. I remembered how much I loved listening to the birds and looking at the clouds. I remembered how good it felt, how necessary, to sit in a room alone and do nothing and talk to no one. In the morning, I remembered the people in my dreams, the colors, the places we went, the things we did, the deliciousness. I remembered how, when I was a child, I had started on a golden path to find my own answers, to find peace.

It was 1980, and I was living in a house with my girlfriend, Siri Narayan, in a two-story yellow Victorian in Berkeley. I had finally found my yellow house. I had met Siri at UCLA, and we had fallen in love. We had moved from LA to Berkeley and found a house on Harmony Street (that really was the name). The house had front and back yards with trees, and birds that sang every morning and throughout the day. It had a spirit of a woman around thirty years old who would come into the kitchen in flannel pajamas and sit with me while I was eating breakfast. We put a sign on our front door that read, "Please Do Not Disturb. Meditation and Creation in Progress," and we withdrew from the world. I was writing poetry, painting, and playing music, and she was painting and choreographing dances. What could have been more perfect? If I had been a Christian, I might have said the Lord was blessing me. But I wasn't. I thought it was the universe, the planets and the stars aligning. I thought the universe was like me; it had forgotten who I was for a while, but now it remembered.

Our house was a block away from the Ashby BART station, the commuter train that ran throughout the Bay Area. Every Saturday there was a giant flea market in the parking lot of the station. It was a festival and a carnival with table after table, and booth after booth, and many kinds of music in the air. A drumming circle, reggae, blues, jazz, and new age. There were clothes and crafts of all kinds, new and old. There were different kinds of furniture, woodcarvings, weaving, macramé, pipes, bottles, dishes, ceramics, instruments, books, pieces of scrap metal, food, tools, carpets, artsy creations you might never find anywhere else, and small appliances. There were some booths with antique stuff, and some with new, and some with hand-made, and some with manufactured, and some with ethnic, and some with brand names. There were booths of artisans, painters, yogis, spiritual groups, massage therapists, incense makers, and crystal healers.

I loved crystals and collected them, the way I had loved and collected special pieces of wood and bark, flower petals, and seashells. Almost everyone I knew had amethyst and quartz and believed in energy fields and chakras. At the psychic school I went to, called Heartsong, we compared our crystals and held them and sat in purple circles and opened our chakras as delicately as whispering to butter-flies. We held them in our palms as we read auras and moved them over each other's bodies to heal damaged energy. We sat them in front of us, in lotus postures, as we read each other's past lives.

At home, I burned sage bundles to purify space, and I let my body become sage smoke and enter the cities pulsing in amethyst and rose quartz crystals. I found peace in the cities there, solace. I rested in the stillness of purple and pink light that almost seemed frozen. But it wasn't. It just pulsed slowly, as things often do that have lived for a long time beneath earth. I burned the hardened gum of frankincense and myrrh and washed myself in the scents until Solomon's temples of cedar surrounded me. I played reggae with David. We loved each other's dreadlocks and washed them in the river and sunned ourselves on rocks. We talked and laughed until it was almost evening and his father called him home. I watched candle flames for hours, like I watched the petals of flowers. I conjured spirits I didn't know, and sometimes they got loose in the house and broke things or threw things.

Sometimes a couple of our Rasta friends dropped by our house. They were old Rastas with thick locks and beautiful smiles. They always smelled of frankincense and greeted us with "Give thanks." I would often see Rastas around Berkeley, and sometimes I hung out with them. Some of them were musicians and poets and were usually eager to talk. I would listen to the smooth and punctuated rhythms of their sermons, manifestos, and liturgies and taste the spirits that emanated from them and their words. I was a Rasta myself by then. I had given myself to its vibe. Rastas would say that I was a Rasta from a time before I was born in this body.

When I first saw dreadlocks, I thought, "Oh yeah, now I remember," and I fell in a love I would never fall out of. When I started growing locks, I was at UCLA. I loved the way it felt, the earth growing out of me. The rawness. But back then, in 1977, black Americans hated dreadlocks. It embarrassed them. It reminded them of homeless, "pathetic bums" who were holding the race back. When I was at my bus stop near my house in Culver City, black schoolkids would make fun and throw rocks at me. On the bus, they would laugh and shoot spitballs. The white people would sit so still, looking out the windows, their jaws clenched, almost shaking, pretending not to notice. When I went home to Virginia, my mama would fuss and almost break down in tears. She wanted me to go to church with her on Sundays, but she was so embarrassed that she let me stay at home.

Growing dreadlocks for me was like a monk shaving his head, wrapping himself in an orange robe, and humming "oms." They were like a womb in which I was nurtured, out of which a new me was being born. When I lied down on the floor and closed my eyes and listened to reggae, spirits would drift out of the radio and into my dreadlocks. Spirits of old Jamaican hill folk. Spirits would move into me and take over my eyes. I would be a root and a bone. Solomon and David would shake their dreadlocks and whisper wise secrets. I would lay my head in Queen Sheba's lap and listen to her hum as her long locks fell around my face and sheltered me from the cruelty of the world. I would be a black scent and a wind wrapped in cotton, in burlap. I would be a watcher on a hill drinking fresh water. I would be singing along with Bob Marley, "Grow your dreadlocks / don't be afraid of the wolf pack" and "Come we go chant down Babylon, one more time."

In the purple time, Siri and me were reading about a lot of spiritual paths, and going to hear different spiritual groups and gurus. Some of them we listened to were Swami Satchidananda, Yogananda, Swami Muktananda, and J. Krishnamurti, and we sometimes ate at the Hare Krishna temple and heard talks by people who didn't have big names or followings. I had started down this path in high school and college when I got involved with a spiritual/therapy group, then Zen, then Buddhist groups, then Baha'is. My granny had helped me to start seeking. She had told me stories about the old days when the young people in our community had to "seek." They would dress in white and go out into the woods alone and wait on their vision. They would stay out there until the vision came, until they were new and bathed in light. She would sometimes shout out of nowhere, startling me, "You need to be seeking your soul salvation!" Since childhood, I had been seeking and seeking. But I wasn't looking for Jesus. I was looking for the perfect moment, the perfect light. So I had read a lot, and thought a lot, and in the purple time, I read and thought a lot more.

Siri and me were thinking that we would find a path we both liked and could be on together. I met lots of people on different paths, and I had friendships. But somewhere, in the back of my mind, I knew I was like a black engine with its piston pumping almost fast enough for me to take flight, or to fall apart. Even in the purple time, when I could relax some, I couldn't slow the motion inside me; I couldn't slow the momentum of my life or the rhythm of my heart. So I was part of those around me, but I wasn't. Some of them were so settled in themselves, in where they were living and what they believed. They weren't used to running, hiding, or falling apart. I was determined to keep holding on to Siri, though, to the purple time, to the yellow house.

But one day I met Rajneesh sannyasins, dressed all in red, with their beads and their malas. One day I tasted their scent, and it tasted like home. One day I was reading a book of Rajneesh lectures, and suddenly my search was over, but Siri's was still going.

When I declared that I had to go to the commune, the life we had together was over. It's funny how things can sometimes end, just like that.

Siri was frightened for me going to the Ranch. Like everyone I knew, she was terrified. They were thinking about Jim Jones and the mass suicides at Jonestown. They were scared I would end up drinking poison Kool-Aid and dying. I had to put up a wall in my mind to keep from hearing what people said. To keep from feeling their anxieties. Once the wall was up, things were quiet and I could think better.

Siri was trying to talk to me because she was upset, but I just wanted to get away from her feelings. So my feelings ran away. When my feelings run away, I am left alone in a wilderness, like a slave who was headed north and suddenly there are no stars. Even worse, there is no sky and I can't remember anything. Why am I here in this field? I hear dogs barking. Trees turn to wolves. So I turn into a wolf and bite anything that comes near me.

That's what I did with Siri, so she thought I had stopped loving her, when I just wanted to go to Rajneeshpuram. I *needed* to, and I was scared. I couldn't think about two things at once, and I was thinking about going. So I couldn't think about Siri's feelings. I needed her too much to leave her, but she didn't know that. So she left me. She left me and went to Yogi Bhajan. She left me and became a Sikh. She dressed all in white, with a turban. She left me and got married and went to live in an ashram. She got up every morning and meditated, while I disappeared in red, into burnt henna, into sannyas, into a mystic rose.

When I was going to Oregon, I was fleeing a yellow house. I was as lost as a kitten. I was a black man, in a purple time, in a green Plymouth Valiant, out in the cold. I was like my daddy sitting in his blue DeSoto, belonging nowhere. I went with a friend from my psychic school, and we left on a Monday because "Monday" is red and we were going to a place that was as bright red as a blossom. She made homemade muesli. I filled the tank with gas, and we found some sleeping bags. That's all the planning we thought of. Early Monday morning, we took off in my Plymouth Valiant, my reggae boat, headed to Rajneeshpuram.

The first night on the road, we slept on a beach. We fell asleep to the *shhhhhhhh* of waves breaking on wet sand and withdrawing back into the sea, to a sky full of stars. I was a little nervous but so excited. I had forgotten that there were any other choices, that there were any other roads. I seemed to belong nowhere I had ever been, with no one I had ever met, doing nothing I had ever seen anyone do. So what did I have to lose?

Late the next day, when we got near the Ranch, I could feel a deep silence with skin I didn't know I had. I could taste it. Touch it. It was as if my sixth sense stepped out of me, like a person of its own. Then it faced me down and moved back into me and took me over.

At the gates of Rajneeshpuram were guards with machine guns. When I saw them, I had to work hard not to have a seizure. I was afraid of guns. There were more guards perched on the surrounding hills. It was like going through a checkpoint in a dark spy movie, crossing the border from one country to another. I hadn't expected the tenseness or surveillance. Once I was inside, I didn't think much more about it, but I felt it, with the hair on the back of my neck. I put myself in take-in mode. Watch. Watch. Taste. Touch. Feel. I could turn on think-about-it mode sometime later. I wouldn't know for a while anyway all the things there were to think about.

I didn't know what to make of the Ranch, a new-age city in the middle of nowhere, kind of like in a science-fiction movie. It wasn't just the things, like the buses, all of the buildings and roads. Dairy farm. Vegetable farm. Honeybees. Meditation hall. Airport. Sewage plant and reservoir. Fire department and boutiques. Restaurants and mall. It wasn't just the new-age stuff like crystal readings, massage, aromatherapy, and chakra balancing. It was the vibe. It was the way sannyasins were in their bodies. Their movements were different from people on the outside. Like the movements of people in movies are different when they are taken over by aliens. The movements here were more relaxed, freer, more alive. But sometimes "crazy religious" people seem that way. I would just have to keep my senses and mind open and see.

I felt the Ranch first with my eyes. Everything was red. Everyone wore shades of red. I could even close my eyes and feel the redness. It was like being inside a giant rose. And the aroma of the rose surrounded us, like the dust of the brown hills. It was the scent of all those who had ever meditated. Delicate, but unmovable. I was inside it. I could feel its heart beat. When sannyasins moved along paths and roadways, the ochers, rubies, scarlets, carmines, crimsons, cerises, vermilions, rouges, russets, auburns, hennas, maroons, magentas, puces, fuchsias, lilacs, plums, lavenders, and mauves of their shirts and pants, skirts and hats, socks and even shoes, were like petals of the blossoms we were inside of. Moving in wind. Dropped in a winding stream.

Every day after lunch there were drive-bys. They were a little weird, but I stayed open. The shades of red would line the roads of Rajneeshpuram. It was an intensity that even the greatest painters would shy away from. Thousands of red lips. Thousands of red petals. Singing and playing tambourines. Swaying to universal "oms." "Oh, Bhagwan, take me high as the eagle fly!" And Bhagwan would come along, driving slowly, slowly, in one of the many Rolls-Royces that rich sannyasins had given him, smiling. He would stop often and move his hands up and down, as much dancing as his aging body could manage. But that was enough to send the sannyasins near his car into rapture. Some of them reminded me of black women in church, struck with the Holy Ghost. The procession would last over an hour, and then everyone would slowly disperse. The blue of the sky would then have more space to spill back into the landscape.

I felt the Ranch secondly with taste. The taste of dust, of sagebrush, of the surrounding brown hills. There was a dryness that lingered on my tongue, on my skin, despite the sweat that gathered as I moved here and there in the heat. And there was a taste of redwood that seemed to get inside me. Redwood was in some of the buildings. I could touch it. It was so soft that I had to be careful not to leave any imprint. It was soft like bacon that had been overcooked and could fall apart from too much handling. It was soft like water, like pinesap before it hardens. There was the taste of new lumber. Of pine, of cedar, in the small A-frame lodges, or in the co-ed bathrooms and showers. There was the taste of soaps and sweat and rosemary oil that sannyasins used to "feed" their meditation beads. There was the taste of the all-vegetarian meals in the cafeteria. Of lots of brown rice, tofu, and tahini.

The third way I felt the Ranch was with touch. Things felt right. All the patterns of paths and gardens felt right. They felt right to my feet. They felt right to my hands as I walked along and touched a leaf, or a wooden railing, a doorknob, a bench, the headboard of the bed, the cotton of the bedspread, the arms of a chair. The angles of rooms, of buildings. The closeness and distance of one thing and another. The shapes things made together—the buildings, bridges, groves, gardens. The stone Buddhas and lanterns. The sparse beauty of Zen texture everywhere I turned. Everywhere was named for an enlightened person. Buddha Hall. Lao Tzu Grove. Jesus Grove. And so each nook had its own light, its own texture, its own spirits. I could almost have closed my eyes, the way I did at home, and moved around and been all right.

Sannyasins touched a lot. Instead of talking most of the time, like people on the outside did, they tried to stay tuned in to an inner silence. I could go for days with only a few words. That was like being in heaven. When people passed on the paths going from here to there, we sometimes hugged and melted into each other. We hugged into the silence that filled the air like water in a jar, and after a while, sometimes a long while, we parted, wordlessly, with a smile. That was like being in heaven too. Quietly holding and being held.

The Ranch was like a school, without gray concrete. Someone had asked, "What is a building?" and gotten a different answer than the people who build gray concrete. These were rooms that breathed like cedar and redwood. I loved those kinds of buildings. They suited my spirit. And what is a building for? To capture space, to mix it with light and shadows. It's like diving into the ocean, and while you're underwater, taking a bucket, or a cup, or a pretty box, and letting it fill up. When I went into buildings with wood, I could hear the trees still talking. The rooms would let the inside light and space rise up like music and put their fingers on the glass and walls to feel the heartbeat of space outside. Timber framing and open beams rested in each other's arms and locked fingers.

Some museums were like that. So the artwork and the trees could talk to each other. So people who went there could stand in the spaces where light and lightness met and be baptized. Lodges where new-age therapy groups met for retreats, meditated, talked about feelings, cried, hugged, and ate vegetarian lunches were like that. They usually had trees outside the windows and nearby saunas or yurts. They had prisms or crystals hanging at windows and breaking light into rainbows. They had smoothly polished hardwood floors. Like the places I went to study yoga or breathwork or tai chi, or to get a cosmic massage. The places I went to get my homeopathy or get my tarot cards or my astrological chart read. The places I went to get the lines in my palm translated into the past and future. There were always soft voices and friendly faces in those buildings and rooms. There was always a sweet scent. People in there left the colors around their bodies open so that I could taste them.

In the school of Rajneeshpuram, I meditated, read, and fell more deeply into my nature. The books were discourses Bhagwan had given over the years. There were hundreds of them, going back to the first ashram in Pune. I couldn't put them down. They were the books I would never find another person to talk to about. My favorites were Bhagwan's *The Book of Secrets*; *My Way, the Way of the White Clouds*; *Journey Toward the Heart: Discourses on the Sufi Way*; and *Only One Sky: On the Tantric Way of Tilopa's Song of Mahamudra*. There were books on Patanjali's yoga sutras, Rumi's Sufism and whirling dervishes, Zen masters, Kabir's poetry, Gurdjieff's experiments with consciousness, Lao Tzu and Chuang Tzu. When Bhagwan spoke, he brought them back into this world. He was like a conjurer. He opened a portal and one by one and they came through. He called it the "Buddhafield," a place where spirits of the enlightened could walk the earth again. It was so quiet in the Buddhafield, like being among the stars.

To people outside, Rajneeshpuram was just a weird place among the weirdnesses of the 1980s. But the silences, the sparks, the textures of life that held it together weren't in the twentieth century at all. People outside were saying a lot of things about the Ranch, most of them not very good. It would turn out that some of those things were true. But I wasn't paying any mind to what people were saying. I was tasting the things that were goodness and light, things that could sustain me.

Instead of going to class, I went to meditations three times a day. In a quiet room, with open wood, and soft pink pillows, I sat like a lotus and hummed while Buddhas floated beside me. Instead of studying for exams, I read for the sake of my soul. Instead of listening to lectures, I sat among the red flock of thousands and breathed in Bhagwan's radiance and a quiet that there is no word for. We knelt and chanted, "Buddham Sharanam Gachchhami / Sangham Sharanam Gachchhami / Dhammam Sharanam Gachchhami," prostrating our heads and hands to the floor at the end of each triplet. Instead of falling into an anxious river at night, and waking up out of breath from fighting white rapids and dog paddling in chilly waters, the way I did when I was in school, I slept. At night I would lie down and fall into a river of blue silence. I would float without effort. I would never completely awaken from it. The tea of Buddha sleep. The nothingness of sleeping, while awake, like rain when the sun is shining. There was a space that imagination cannot bridle. That became solid. There was a brightness that did not blind my eyes or give me headaches. That did not answer to the sun.

I had read about and seen pictures of monks in orange robes. But I had never seen them up close. It was so foreign. But it was even more familiar. It felt so right. I wished that I could have stayed on the Ranch or in another of the ashrams. I wished that I could have just kept living with the Buddhas. I would have been at home. But, "If it's for you," my granny would say, "you'll get it." What I had were debts and loans to pay back, so I would have to find a job and work. I was desperate to "take sannyas," to become a sannyasin, because I knew my time was short. I knew that at any minute, I could be sucked back into the world. Like in a movie when a part of an airplane is blown apart and passengers are sucked screaming into the sky. Bhagwan told the story once of a disciple who reached the fifth heaven, stayed there for a while, and then fell back into the world. When you fall back this time, he said, don't forget. Remember your selves. Remember to meditate.

Since I couldn't stay, I would have to take it with me, like I did most things I cared for, on the run. All the rivers of love. All the light. All the amazing sensitivity, to senses, to the planet, to the forces of the universe. All the beautiful words: Samadhi. Moksha. Enlightenment. Satori. Satsang. I would have to take the idea that each of us has to find our own peace. That no religion or doctrine can give it to us. I would carry it in my heart, along with the other precious things. The red. The reds. All the reds.

They didn't let me take sannyas the first time I was at the Ranch. They said I wasn't ready. They said I needed to meditate for three months and then come back. And I did. I was doing Dynamic, Kundalini, and Nadabrahma meditations at least twice every day, in the morning, at noon, and in the evening. Nadabrahma was my favorite. It was based on a Tibetan meditation. I sat and hummed to the music of Tibetan gongs, then slowly opened my arms to the universe, and then slowly folded them. I was like a blossom, opening then closing. By the end of Nadabrahma, I was alive with such a silence. I was myself before the traumas, before I learned despair.

When I returned to the Ranch, they said I was ready to melt and I could take sannyas. There was a large open building called Buddha Hall where Osho (he changed his name from Bhagwan) sat on a platform, facing sometimes as many as a thousand sannyasins. When we took sannyas, our names were called and we walked up to the front where someone handed us a page with our new names and what the names meant and put the mala around our necks. The mala had 108 rosewood beads, each one for a different kind of meditation. It had Osho's picture in round, hardened clear plastic at the bottom. It was like being baptized.

When I took sannyas, I was so happy. My happiness is the main thing I remember. I don't know what day or month it was, or what I was wearing, or anything else about that time when I was on the Ranch. It felt so familiar that I never doubted its truth. Its value. I never doubted that I had been with Osho in some other life. I remembered his taste. I remembered how much I loved him. I was happy to be rejoining so many familiar souls. I was happy to know I was sharing my journey. I was happy to have positive routines to help guide me. Meditations helped to center me, to lessen the times when my mind slipped away. They were like medicine. Of all the things I've learned, meditation has been one of the most important. Learning to meditate was a turning point. Without it, I don't know how I would have survived. The university degrees wouldn't have saved me. They wouldn't have centered me or given me inner refuge in the storms of life.

My new name was Swami Anand Prahlad. Swami meant a committed meditator. "Anand" meant "bliss," and "Prahlad" meant "joy." All men sannyasins were Swamis, and all women were Mas. Inside, I was secretly a Swami-Ma. Out of all the sannyasins, there were only a few second names. "Anand" was one of them. "Anand" was the path of the desert, which was finding oneself in solitude.

I was used to my new name right away, but it would take people who already knew me time. My mama was so insulted. "What's wrong with the name I gave you?" She almost cried. A woman from our church said, to comfort Mama, "This too shall pass." But I was thinking, *Oh no it won't*. I was thinking how it's funny that people assume the things they don't like will pass. But what about the things they do like? What about my first name, Dennis? What about Christianity?

I Think I Do

I'm sitting here wondering/if a matchbox will hold my clothes.
– Blind Lemon Jefferson

There were times when I had no structures to keep me together. Those times it was often difficult to function. It was harder to remember things. I had more blank-outs. I couldn't get a hold of time. After I took sannyas and returned to the Bay Area was one of those times. I had no job. No steady relationship. For the first time in my life, I wasn't writing. Meditation had taken the knots out of my belly that had fed my poetry. I sometimes didn't have an apartment or house to live in, and I was often lost somewhere for days. I sometimes couldn't find my mind to think what to do, and so I slept in my car. There was nowhere to take a shower and so I got really dirty.

I had an Ethiopian Rasta friend named Girma who let me stay at his house for a few days. I loved Girma. He was gentle and happy. He doted on me. I awoke at Girma's to the sounds of Ethiopian piano and smells of spicy foods.

Some days I went from Berkeley to San Francisco, just because I didn't know where else to go. There were days when I was walking on the street and suddenly my mind would disappear and I couldn't remember why I was there, where I was, or how to get home. I would be like two sheets in the wind that had come loose from the clothesline, blowing wherever.

I was lucky to sometimes attract nice people who would help me. A few times a woman would come along when I was lost, and she would smile at me, and she would smell good, and she would be radiant. She would start talking to me, and the sound of her voice would be so soothing, I would have followed her anywhere. And then she would hold out her hand and I would take it. We would take a bus, or a cable car, or we would walk a long way up some hills, and the traffic would be singing and other people would be walking too or standing at bus stops or coming out of shops. She would sometimes talk, and the wind would blow pieces of shade back and forth. And I would talk, and I would get lost in the warm space of our voices going back and forth like the shade. I would forget everything else. Sometimes we wouldn't get where we were going until it was evening and the night jasmine was making everyone along the sidewalks as drunk as bees. It would feel like another time in another world, and I would feel safer and warmer having someone with me.

One time she was a hippie with an Indian skirt. I had a weakness for hippies in Indian skirts. One time she was a teller from the financial district. One time she was a trans girl from the red-light district. One time she didn't speak much English, only Portuguese. At those apartments, I saw the rooftop view of San Francisco, an endless membrane of lights pulsing like an embryo. I saw a garden of calla lilies beside green chairs. Sometimes apartments were at the tops of wooden stairs in old Victorians, like in a movie or in a dream when the stairway ends before I reach the top. One time an apartment had a red sofa and a painting of Frida Kahlo. I loved Frida Kahlo. One apartment had metal chairs and a glass coffee table. One had a radio, and one had a black television. Some of the women made food for me. Sometimes strangers can be the best friends—often, in my life. They were all so nice and so tender. I liked sleeping with them and touching warm legs to legs, and smelling the shampoo of their hair and lotions on their skin.

In the middle of the night, one woman got up and said, "I'll be right back, baby." There was a lot of noise, and when she opened the door to go into the living room, I saw two other women passing a crack pipe and two men with guns. I heard Lowell Fulson singing "Reconsider Baby," which made me think of my daddy, because it was one of his favorite songs. I heard a lot of *bitches* and *motha'fuckas*, and then the woman came back. Her name was Princess. She sat on the bed and took my head in her hands and said, "I want you to listen to me. OK? Listen to me. I've got to go take care of something. Don't you scream. Just don't go there. I know you having a hard time with the noise. I had a brother like you, so I know, all right, baby? I'm goin' to be back. So just find something to count. You like counting things, don't you? My brother used to count the clicks of the fan. If anybody comes in here, you're my brother from Detroit, OK." And then she smiled and said, "You ol' donkey dong." And then, "You know I don't mean nothin' by it, don't you?" I held on to her pillows when she left. Don't worry. I wasn't worried. I was tired. Jeremiah and Lizzy hugged me, and I fell back to sleep.

I liked sleeping with people sometimes. It could make me feel safe, like when I slept with my sisters and brothers as a child. Of all the people in my life, the ones I remember best are those I've slept with. Most of them had nothing to do with sex. I think I remember them because the sentry comes down off the wall of the fort. The world slows down and gets quiet, so I can focus on the other person. I can see more clearly who they are. I think I remember them because I counted their breaths. I put the colors of their heartbeats in a red velvet satchel. And I remember them because sometimes I have seizures in my sleep, and the people who have held me as I was coming back are like family.

But some days when I went to San Francisco, things didn't go very well. Like, this one orange day in the city, I was parked on a hill downtown and my car overheated. I remember the sound of the traffic, like a river of water overflowing, coming over the hill and roaring down. I opened the hood to take a look and started to open the radiator. I was untwisting the cap slowly, the way I had seen mechanics do, but something grabbed my attention. The sound of an engine. The beautiful view of the marina in the distance. Hot water gushed from the radiator, pouring onto my chest and face.

My body was burning, and I was tearing off my shirt. But before I could get it off, the water had burned the cotton into the skin of my chest and stomach. I had never felt that kind of pain. I walked back and forth, crying. I sat down on the sidewalk. I sat in my car and screamed. When I could think, I drove back to Berkeley, to my friend Aimee's house. Aimee was a good friend. We had so many good conversations about the passages and colors of our lives. One time we spent the day sitting in a field, reading, and I was playing music, and we were not talking. We were just clouds.

After I got burned, I stayed in bed at Aimee's house, on fire, while for days she brought me water and changed the dressings. My skin was pink, but not the pink of a flower. Nothing is really pink like human flesh when it opens up from burns. I probably should have gone to the hospital, but I didn't think about it. Sometimes now when I look in the mirror and see the scars, the patches where the color of my skin never came back, I remember the view of the marina. I remember Aimee taking care of me, and I start jumping around nervously, as if I'm on fire.

Eventually, I found my way to sannyasin households. One of them was a yellow house in Berkeley. People in red were coming and going to and from the yellow house, and my green Valiant was parked on the street outside. The house belonged to Ma Prem Svarna, an American sannyasin. It had a flower garden and a quiet backyard. I could tell that some of the sannyasin boisterousness bothered Svarna. Before sannyas, she was probably living alone, had a few good friends, went to a good job every day, and came back home. It hurt her to see her quiet yellow house turned into a social hub, sometimes into a circus. But she was learning the lesson of letting go.

I met a lot of sannyasins living in Svarna's house. A European sannyasin named Ma Prem Mano lived there with her two children, Kuba and Karina. She was one of those who had been with Bhagwan since the early days in Puna, India. She told me a lot of stories about the early days. Mano was a "house ma," a center of the networks of sannyasins in the Bay Area. So our house was like a heart, and I liked living close to the heartbeat. I could know about everything that was going on without leaving home. I loved the feeling of belonging to a family and being surrounded day and night by sensitive people, by shades of red. I met sannyasins from Ethiopia,

Germany, England, the Netherlands, India, Italy, Sweden, France, Japan, Korea, and other places. I had soft friends, some who could barely speak English.

But, inside, I was drowning. I couldn't focus, because I had no routine or structure. Sannyasin relationships were like streams of water, flowing all of the time. How well we could flow was supposed to be a measure of our commitment to Bhagwan. But I was already water. I needed land. And that was the moment when I met my first wife.

Her name was Ma Prem Pravahi, and we were together for a few weeks before she became pregnant. And so we got married, early in the morning, in a meadow in a wilderness, with a few friends, with a garland like hippies wore. Birds were singing and a boom box was playing *Pachelbel's Canon*. I was thinking about the dew in the meadow where I was born and about the little green trailer. "I do," we said. I do. I think I do.

I moved into my wife's house on Twenty-Fourth Street in the Mission District of San Francisco. I loved the Mission District. It was a sunny valley, with mostly people of Hispanic descent. It felt like I was in South America. It was warmer and quieter than most parts of the city, because the hills around it buffered us against the cool breezes and a lot of the noises of the city.

I moved out of living in streams and into living on land. I walked out of the water like the first animal. I was soaking wet. The light was too bright. Everything was too noisy. The food tasted strange. Every object was too hard to touch. Every movement was hard. There was something called time that ran people, like hunters run deer. But it was invisible. I liked some things about the land, but I kept dreaming of going back into the water.

We should have talked about things, but we didn't. We were caught up in the excitement and energy of the sannyasin movement. We knew each other's spirits, or vibes, but that was not nearly enough. We couldn't have been more different. She liked to go out all of the time, and the house was just a place to sleep and eat. She measured life by the number of social interactions in a day. I liked to stay at home. I measured life by the number of silences.

I had no idea what she wanted, or who she really was, and she had no idea what I wanted or what I was thinking. I thought that since we were both sannyasins, we would think the same things. I was thinking that we would keep being sannyasins and that we would keep having lots of sannyasins at our house. I was thinking that our relationship would be open. I hadn't thought at all about things like going to work or paying the bills. I was thinking that I was still black as ever, because I was. I was thinking that I was still very much a Rasta. I was thinking of financially getting by, because that's all I had ever known. She was thinking that the open-house sannyasin life was over and that we would start being the all-American family. She was thinking that me being a new-age person meant I wasn't really black. She was thinking that I must have as much wealth as she did. She was thinking we would be living the good life because that's what she was used to.

We got along well for the few weeks before she became pregnant. Before we were living together or being serious about the future. But after that, there were no more good times. We went to a therapist, but the therapist was also a white sannyasin. She didn't know anything about black people either, or about autism or Asperger's (a word I didn't know yet). I never felt we were talking about the real issues, but I wasn't able to articulate what those issues were. My feelings had already scattered to the four winds. My feelings had run out of my belly and were hiding in abandoned warehouses, under bridges and in overgrown fields. They would only appear sometimes when I was alone with our son.

But even if my feelings had been there, in the therapy sessions, they couldn't have expressed themselves. My wife and the therapist built a house with the way they spoke. The way they took deep breaths between sentences. The way they frowned or smiled. But it was not a house my feelings could breathe in. It was a house without the right colors that my feelings could make into words. It was a house the color of a gray day. Each session, I meant to say, *I don't think this is going to work. I don't think this is going to make any difference.* But the conversation would roll along, like a go-cart going down a hill. The clock ticked. I felt bad for my wife. I felt bad for the therapist. I felt bad for them because they wanted so badly to make everything about white lights and radiance that they couldn't see all the other shades of the world. They couldn't see simple things, like sometimes two people just aren't meant to be together.

After our son was born, I had to learn about practical things, like money, and work, and cars, and being a parent. I went back to school for a primary/secondary teaching certificate. I started teaching at Golden Gate Elementary School in Oakland Unified School District. Once I started teaching in Oakland, I got up at five o'clock every morning and drove to work. At three o'clock, when school was out, I drove to Haywood State University to take evening classes. Coming home late at night, I had to cross the San Mateo-Hayward bridge, a seven-mile stretch of darkness that linked San Francisco to the East Bay. I would be fighting sleep, nodding off behind the wheel and dreaming of plummeting over the rail, sinking down into the waters. That would evoke a feeling of being cold, of freezing, and shivering would help to keep me awake. I would imagine our house as a light in a dark forest, which, when I reached it and went in, would be filled with warmth and love and security. When I got home, though, it was never that way. The next day, I would forget the night before and imagine the same thing all over. I needed the image in order to keep going, even if I knew it wasn't true.

Things were bad for me in our house. There was no quiet, no space. And me and my wife didn't seem to be friends. Friends are nice to each other. They want each other to be happy. They say "How are you doing?" or "What's the matter?" They don't take each other's dignity. They don't fight all the time.

My wife knew the language of fighting, but I didn't. Her father had taught it to her. For them, fighting was part of love. But I had been taught that it was wrong to fight, and especially, you should never say or do anything bad to your child's other parent. A mother was special. Sacred. So was a committed father. And so I often said nothing. But saying nothing seemed to make it worse.

And besides, no one could win a fight with me. It was never fair because I never played by the rules. Ever since I was a child, I had a knack for driving people crazy. Everybody said it, even if they loved me. Just my difference was sometimes irritating to people. They thought I was trying to be difficult, or that I was just cruel. They were arguing with something I couldn't feel. With meanings that were foreign. With contracts I hadn't signed. I was responding to their meanings with colors. With my logic. With the right places for things. With symmetry. With tastes.

I knew I was the being of blue, of light blue, like the sky. I knew I was the chapter of blue. I was to spread light blue, like a flower or a butterfly. So usually I blew soft blue words to people because it made them happy, even though they didn't see the blue words any more than they see spirits.

Sometimes in arguments, though, I would blow red words at people. Sometimes I would blow red whispers at different parts of their bodies, and watch them come undone. I could be the Dennis the Menace my parents named me after without meaning to be. When I blew red words at people, they would get so mad they couldn't see straight. They would be ready to explode. They would want to hit me, and sometimes I would be terrified, like I was when Daddy took off his belt and got ready to whip us. I would be feeling like I was something small being attacked by giants. Like Brer Rabbit, running from Brer Bear.

I have had girlfriends who tried to stab me. Or to set me on fire. Or to run me over with their car. Or to turn the gas stove on when I was sleeping. Or to kick me out of their car, hours away from civilization, and leave me. They weren't Robert Johnson's black blues women, poisoning him. Or Al Green's soul women throwing hot greens on him. Or the insane. Or psychopaths. They were middle-class, educated, mostly white women. But it wasn't just my girlfriends I drove crazy. It was also friends and people I didn't know. I've had waiters, storeowners, and people working in stores go into fits and embarrass themselves, throw things, or break their own glass counters in response to conversations with me.

People would be wanting to touch something solid when they talked or argued. But there would be nothing but atmosphere, with the occasional yellow blur of a canary.

Truth came up a lot in yellow houses. Like my wife would say, "Just tell the truth," and I would usually say nothing, or say whatever I thought would make her happy. I would be thinking, *I've heard that one before.* I would want to just get back to having a good feeling. I would be looking at the faces in the wood of stair railings, cabinets, a coffee table, the floors. I would be looking at the angles of the room and thinking how amazing they were. I would be looking at the light coming in a window. The truth was that I didn't know what the truth about my feelings was. My feelings would be lost, and I wouldn't be able to find them. They were used to running, to foraging. To alleys and fields. They didn't really know how to live in a yellow house. It took so little to scare them into bolting away, and they disappeared so fast that I had to struggle to get them to come back. To get them to come back could take a long, long time.

The truth was that being in a relationship was like being in a rich person's house. I was seldom at ease. I was always afraid I was going to break something, ruin something, or do or say the wrong thing.

Did I love her, my wife would ask. Did I want to be with her? Was I committed? Or she would say, "You don't really love me" or "You don't want to be with me." I had heard other partners say the same things. I knew those were supposed to be easy questions, but they weren't. I didn't know how to know those things. I didn't know where to get the answers from. By the time I knew what I felt or thought about something, it was usually too late to do anything about it.

"Are you cheating on me?" she would ask. "Tell the truth." And I would start thinking about my secrets and wondering if they equaled cheating. Beware of "firsts," the books say about people on the autism spectrum. They never get past them. I never did. My first lessons were all secrets.

The first secret was when I was molested in the barn as a child.

The second secret was when I was molested at the doctor's office. Sometimes, while I was facing the wall or lying facedown on the cot with my pants down, waiting to get a shot, the nurse's hands searched for something under my skin. Her breath changed and she inhaled deeply. The freckles on her arm turned to water and washed over me. The water was warm. Eventually, she turned me around and looked at my body and smoothed the skin of my hips like smoothing out a tablecloth. I could feel her hands and her eyes long after we had left. Even lying in bed, sick, the feelings would come to me. The waves of her freckles would wash over me.

The third secret was the books of pictures I carried in my mind since I was in elementary school. Pictures of surprise moments. They were like the seedpods I kept, or the birds' nests or pieces of bark. They comforted me and helped the world to stay balanced. Once, in elementary school, Janet Jones turned around in her seat, and her smile was so sweet it never left me. Once, one of my cousins was swinging high on a swing set and I saw her panties against the dark skin of her thighs. They had strawberries on them. I would think about them a lot when I had headaches, or when my head was spinning from too many sounds or too many colors or too much brightness. It was just like eating cold strawberries.

The fourth secret was when I was young and secretly playing doctor with my cousin. There was a summer when she came to get me almost every day. The hollyhocks were blooming bright pink beside my granny's house. Butterflies clustered around wisteria. We'd sneak away to a cool spot beneath pines, or to a hidden room of Granny's house. My cousin would lie down and say very sternly, "Now say it. Say it." She would slap me and then apologize and hold my head in her hands. "Say it, say it!" she would insist again, and I would pretend to be the doctor. "Let's take these down," I'd say in the pretend voice. "Don't worry. I just need to do a little exam. Let me look at your privates."

"Privates" was like a magic word. It changed our breaths.

The fifth secret was that boys sometimes turned into girls. I saw boys turn in elementary school. I sometimes did it myself. Many times, I wished that I had male and female genitals and breasts. I felt like I had both. I loved girl things since I was a child. It started with my mama and my granny. I loved being in Mama and Daddy's room. I loved all the smells of lotions and perfume and powders and Noxzema.

One of my favorite places was their closet. There were so many dresses and skirts and shirts with so many color tones and textures. When I went in there, they would rub against my skin, against my arms and face, and sometimes one would break the secret code of objects and reach out for me. I would hold my hands out, or my face, and close my eyes, and let it caress me. Mama left a lot of herself in the closet. When I was in there, I could see into her better. I could see her happiness when I looked in her pink hatbox.

At a summer camp for student leaders, I met another boy who turned into a girl. He went around in the barracks at night acting tough and pulling the covers off boys who were sleeping and hitting them across their butts really hard with a belt. For me, the belt triggered memories of getting beaten by my daddy. When I fell apart, and pleaded with the boy to stop, he said OK and told me to meet him the next day in our barracks.

The next day he sat beside me on the bed and turned into a girl. He held my hand and said, "I'm sorry." And then we lay down and he held me like I was a girl. He rubbed nappy hair against my face. We didn't talk. I could hear the din of voices outside, coming from different distances and directions. Diffused light broke through small, opaque windows on one wall, close to the ceiling. I could hear her breath get very heavy as she moved against me, and then it got calmer, and me and Ruby were happy.

The sixth secret was the first time I had sex. There was a white girl in science lab in high school named M. When we stood at long, high tables to do experiments, like cutting open pigs or frogs, or mixing chemicals together, she was usually to my right. Sometimes she smiled at me and needed help with something, so I helped her. But one time when I was helping her, I caught her scents. First, there was the patchouli splashed on her neck. And then I smelled her strawberry shampoo, but also her hair, and the scent of the pillows she slept on. Baby powder deodorant was a subtle spice in the stronger, salty wind of her armpit sweat. I could smell the house where she lived, and the thin resin of Dove soap coating her body. I could smell the ripples of heat rising from beneath her skirt.

The rest of the day, I couldn't talk. If anyone said anything to me, I didn't even hear it, or I snapped at them. I snapped hard, like I did as a child, wanting to cut into them with my voice so that they would leave me alone. When I went back to my place at the science table and I was just standing there, overwhelmed, M had looked over and smiled at me. Did she know what had happened?

After the day that I smelled M, I couldn't stop thinking about her. I couldn't stop tasting her on my tongue. Even when I was eating, sometimes, I would taste her. I kept feeling that my face was buried under her arms, or in her hair, or between her thighs. I wouldn't look at her or talk to her for a while, though. Something from her had entered me, like seeds enter the earth. So I finally decided that I should have sex. I had been studying the polio vaccination and thought that having sex would be like getting an immunization—that once I had it, I would be immune to the constant tensions I was feeling. I would be able to get my focus back.

One night, we went parking and she showed me what to do. Some things about it were interesting, like, people were just like horses and dogs. Like, bodies know how to talk to each other, without us saying a word. Like, the fire and water inside us are older than our minds. And some things about it were good, like, floating in air, without gravity. Like, floating in warm water without a tub. Like, the cry when things run from our bodies like a person from a burning house, and the two bodies almost seem to become one.

But some of it felt bad. Touching breasts gave me a sinking feeling, like when an elevator falls. Having my back touched felt like I was being raped. Having my neck or throat touched was the worst. Taking my pants down reminded me of getting ready for a whipping or being swallowed by the shadow in the barn. And lying on top of another person just seemed ugly and wrong.

The seventh secret was M's pregnancy. We didn't know how she got pregnant, since she was on the pill and I was using a rubber. But she did. And then the eighth secret was her abortion. Her mother secretly sent her away to a clinic in Boston for the procedure.

The ninth secret was the open marriage. M's mother was probably the only white mother in the county who would have allowed a black boy into her home, much less to see her daughter. It had been our secret. But after the abortion, she had a change of heart. She pushed M to marry a "decent" white man, but what she didn't know was that they had agreed to have an "open marriage." Ideas about open marriages and swinging were popular in the sixties. There were cartoons about it in magazines like *Playboy*. So I kept seeing M occasionally for the next three years.

My secrets were always there, in yellow houses. They didn't fade with time. I was always still figuring them out. I was always still finding comfort in the familiarity of their flavors. If I didn't taste them for a while, I became hungry for them, the way I missed my mama's greens and candied yams and corn bread. I missed the forbidden words, the words "polite" people didn't say. But not just the words, the attitude that made them all right and forbidden at the same time, like salt flowing into sugar.

I missed the letting go that "polite" people didn't do. I missed a forbidden, freckled hand. I missed the playing with danger and guilt. I missed the space of no morals, where my wounds could meet the wounds of someone like me and somehow be comforted. I missed the secret scents. I missed boys who turned into girls. I missed lesbians telling me I was a lesbian in a man's body, and holding Ruby, and opening her up. I missed being "over there," looking over here, and laughing at the vanilla side of the street.

Once I was in relationships, I didn't know where to put the secret parts of me. I had learned from childhood not to trust them. They weren't acceptable. My wife was from a world where the only places for those parts of me were closets or cages. It was like that with most of my girlfriends. They were white and knew how the white world worked, even if they disowned it or felt they didn't fit into it. They were straight. They were neurologically typical. They were moral. They had a sense of structure and could communicate and hold jobs. I was so "not normal" that I needed normal people to be with. I would sometimes meet people who were more like me than some of my partners were. I met them among the homeless, or in red-light districts, psych wards, or ashrams. I would taste them when they talked, or when they stood near me. But I didn't want a girlfriend from those worlds. It would have been like the neurotypical leading the neurotypical.

When I was living in all those yellow houses, I never thought about having ASD or what it meant to have it. I didn't know that I carried so many secrets. I didn't even realize that I kept living in yellow houses. I didn't know how I felt a lot of the times. Or what. I remember now, though, because I've had time for my feelings to come back. And because I often feel the same way now. I know that I felt I was really alone and had to take care of myself, even when I was with other people. I knew that other neurotypicals think they're right all the time, and they think the way I am is wrong.

I knew how to take care of myself better than other people knew how to take care of me. I made my own rules all the time, in almost everything. I didn't understand neurotypical rules. Too often they didn't make sense. They wouldn't protect me. I didn't feel like they applied to me. I would never have survived just following neurotypical rules. The same way a black person coming from a plantation wouldn't have survived following white people's rules. But my rules weren't necessarily the best ones to follow in a relationship. For example, my rules said disconnect the minute I'm overwhelmed. Stop listening. Find a good feeling wherever I can whenever I need to. Keep my secrets. Don't bring certain things up because I'd never be able to explain them.

Surviving and being in relationships seemed to be two different things. Surviving and being black with ASD in cross-racial relationships seemed to be many different things.

Gray Concrete

Don't change horses in the middle of the stream.

I went to see a movie about a boy who was on the autism spectrum. It was called *Stand Clear of the Closing Doors*. His sister forgot to pick him up from school, and so he wandered directionless in the city, lost, not realizing the danger he was in, not understanding how time works. A symbol on someone's jacket caught his eye, and he followed it into the subway. Once there, he couldn't get out. He didn't know how to. So he lived there for ten days. The sounds of screeching and loudspeakers, people's voices, the fluorescent lights, the scents, were like knives sticking in his brain. He crouched in a seat on the train, terrified, clinging to himself. He rode train after train, getting off when they shut down at night. Eating from garbage cans. Drinking from subway sinks. He peed on himself, and he got so dirty. But the subway slowly became familiar, even if it was painful to be there. He would rather have been at home, but he couldn't think to get there. So he started to learn the rules of how the trains worked. What to expect. How to find safety.

Concrete buildings have been my subway. I know the rules there. I know the roles. I know how to talk to people in gray concrete. What to say. How much to say. When to say things. Student. Teacher. Patient. Client. The wolf can't huff and puff and blow the buildings down.

There is not a lot of moving around in gray concrete. There is not a lot of expressing emotions. There is no yelling, fighting, or calling names. You don't need to keep time because it is kept for you. You can find time to dream. You can find time to read. Like when I'm waiting for the doctor to come. Or in a classroom waiting for the teacher. When the doctor or the teacher comes, they always smile and say something polite and friendly. There's a minute of talk, but no more. Something real, but not too personal. About seventy words. These are the rules of gray concrete.

Most of the time, I didn't want to go to gray concrete. I wanted to stay at home with my things. Familiar and soft things. The right temperature. The right scents. But I had to go. And getting there was filled with small traumas. First, there was just getting ready. Tearing myself away from the comfort of my mind, where there was no time. And no hurry. And no lines between me and spirits. And nobody else's rules. And no small or capital letters. Suddenly, the clock was a boss, and I was working in the fields. Suddenly, I had to put my glasses on so that I could see the lines between things instead of just the shapes and colors. It hurt my head to focus on the lines. To make edges where there didn't seem to be any. And every time I left home, it was like the first time. It was like tearing pieces of skin from my body.

I always got to gray concrete in cars, or buses, or on trains. I learned to take deep breaths and pretend that nothing was out there. That I didn't know what I knew. That I wasn't going to be crossing a desert. That the distance between home and where I was going was not aflame, was not like a flood zone, a tundra, a forest fire. That I was normal and it would be painless. It would be nothing. Like it was no big deal for other people. The heartaches of horns. The headaches of sirens. The searing of light. The stinging of cold. The burning cold of rain, burying into the cells of my body. The endless groaning and revving of engines. The hidden fury of traffic waves. The nausea of motion and speed.

Sometimes I would be going to the gray concrete where there were doctors. The rooms there were full of hard things, a lot of metal, and air that was too cool. At least it was usually quiet there. A nice person would call my name, and I would stand on a scale. They would wrap a blood pressure cuff around my arm and take my temperature. When the doctor came, she would be trying to clear the last patient she had seen from her mind. She would look distracted for a minute and then start asking me questions. I would try to remember to practice talking, before she came, so that words would come out of my mouth. But still, it took a minute. Question. Answer. Question. Answer. Stethoscope and gentle hands pressing against my chest. My back. Gentle voice, telling me to breathe. Listening. Listening. Rustle of cloth against the paper on the exam table. Hands on either side of my neck, feeling for glands. My doctors have usually been good-mood people. I wondered how they stayed in such a good mood talking to people all day.

Sometimes I would be going to the gray concrete of a hospital. Light-colored concrete, cinder blocks, shades of light green, gray, occasional shades of light yellow. Coldness would emanate from the walls and the floors. Even though they were covered with tiles, or with gray or brown Berber carpet that never really looked clean. They usually had clocks on the wall. Round, ugly brown or black with white faces and arrow hands that clicked but resisted clicking. Sometimes the clocks would have bars around them. Someone was trying to trap time, but they couldn't. They had long hallways, like a train. Like a square tube that gets gradually smaller at the far end. Like a tunnel that leads to other tunnels. Like a maze in a surreal reality. And in the ceilings were sometimes florescent lights. They buzzed and hissed and laughed as you walked beneath them. They flickered and hummed. Mocking light. Mocking balance. Mocking the deliberateness of matter.

The rooms were full of soft things, trying to cover the metal and other hardness. It would be the same every time. I would be in a bed. And they would be putting me to sleep. They would be trying to kill me in order to help me. The anesthesia would never work right, and death would come along and take me into his hands. He would carry me in his arms like a soldier carrying another soldier from the battlefield. My head would open up, and everything inside would lose its place, its meaning. Its sense. Its order. I would still be able to hear the doctors and nurses, talking about my body as if no one was inside. I would still be able to hear the sounds of metal instruments clinking on metal trays. The surgeon's commands. Machines beeping. Liquids dripping, and cool weights moving through my veins. Then, for a long time I would hear nothing. Feel nothing. And then I would be hearing them trying to wake me up. I would hear the panic in their voices. And then I would feel blankets on me, even though I was still cold. I would feel a pillow. I would think, there was a window, and warm light was pouring in, bathing me, even if no window was really there. I would slowly come back, but my mind would not come back for a long time. And nothing in my body would work for months.

Sometimes I would be going to the other kind of hospital. You know. Like the ones for "disturbed" people. There were no metaphors inside this kind of gray concrete. The walls wouldn't let them through. Things inside there were just themselves. Just being inside gray concrete was like taking a sedative or an antidepressant. Everything moved to a low, dull place in the center—there were no edges. There was hardly any taste. But there were soft things on the bed. And there were soft sofas with soft pillows. The building would seem like it was tilted though. So I would have to tilt myself to one side to compensate.

They would give me a different kind of drug there. They might strap me down so I wouldn't harm myself. I would sleep, and sleep, and sleep. Sometimes I would feel hands under my covers at night, under my gown, and a voice in my mind would say, "Just let them have it," and I would be back in the barn or the nurse's office when I was a child. I would hear deep breaths, like the breaths of the horses when they had been running. I would be relieved not to have energy to care. In the morning, I would have to go to group meetings, and the talking sounded like a choir was singing. I would try not to sing or to laugh. I wouldn't know anything from anything else. People from plants or pillows. Day from night. Myself from other patients or spirits. The bathroom from the living room. Food from medicine. My hands from pieces of leather. Paper from metal. I wouldn't know how I got there, or where "there" was, until later when I had gotten out.

Sometimes I went to gray concrete to stand in front of a classroom. Like when I was eighteen and I taught poetry in a room without windows in the Virginia State Penitentiary. It was in the Richmond Poet-in-the-Schools program. Every week, I rode a city bus there. I held on to myself and pretended I was going somewhere exciting, instead of passing through gray, noisy streets filled with smoke. Smoke like that which hovered in the yard back on the plantation where I grew up. And there was nothing soft in prison. Nothing soft, except clothes. It was a nightmare of dark concrete hallways, dimly lit with a blood-colored light. Every night I dreamed of being trapped beneath the rubble of prison concrete, its weight pressing down on my chest until I couldn't breathe. The inmates' sweat followed me into my dreams. The shotguns the guards held. The batons. The pistols. The jangling of their large circle of keys.

Or, when I was in my thirties, I rode the bus in Oakland, California, to gray concrete, to stand in front of more classrooms. Here and there in the city. I was a substitute teacher. Sometimes I changed buses. And changed buses again. I tasted crowds of people packed into trembling seats or standing and holding on for dear life to metal rails and poles. Trying desperately not to see each other or to see themselves. I took deep breath after deep breath when the bus put me off, and I stood before red bricks mortared over concrete. I tried to buffer my ears against the schoolyard noise. I walked down halls where sulfur-colored crowds shimmered in silhouettes, while bluish light tried to splash through windows in the doors at the end. The music of the shadows was a familiar joviality. But the humming of the shadows was a pain I had never known.

I would enter classrooms and light would split my head. I would sit behind desks and be invisible as the wind. Nothing soft. Nothing soft. The talking around me would never seem to stop. There were so many different voices. So many different tones. So many different pitches, cadences, and anxious sounds like foot tapping, and shuffling, and one hand pinching the skin of the other hand, or hands tugging on elastic socks or waistbands all at once. It would make me dizzy. I would be drowning in the scents. Grease and burnt toast. Scrambled eggs and beans. The mix of soap and water, urine and foot funk, shower mold, sweat and underarms. Powder and cologne. Deodorant and perfumes. Peppermint and lotions. Listerine. I had to hold onto myself to keep from vomiting. I would have to put my hand on the back of my head to keep my head from exploding. I would have to hold tightly to the corner of the desk and the chairs and look straight ahead to keep from having a seizure. I would be holding it together so people would think I was normal. So they would think I was one of them. And then, the loud bells would ring.

I would be so confused about the rules. They were nothing like the ones I had learned for school. None of the rules I had learned about classrooms in gray concrete seemed to apply. Sometimes students just all got up and started leaving. I tried to talk to them, but no one seemed to hear me. I followed them out to the playground, calling, but no one turned around. I watched them fanning out, disappearing past cars and down sidewalks in different directions. When they had all vanished, everything was so quiet. I could hear a bird singing. I stood there for a little while, waiting to see if they would come back. But they didn't.

Sometimes teachers would lock themselves in classrooms at recess, afraid to come out. Or they would be afraid that if they said anything to certain students, someone would slash their tires. Students would be doing so many things they shouldn't have been doing in a classroom. And I would be helpless to stop them. Playing card games at the back of the room. Playing their boom boxes. Dancing or getting into fights. I couldn't stop them from doing anything. I couldn't suspend anyone. I couldn't even send them to the office. I couldn't bring them out of their shock. I couldn't make them believe in another world. I couldn't scream, even when I felt like it.

And if I could have gotten their attention, what should I have told them? Maybe it helps at times if you don't have autism when you're a teacher. If life seems to make sense to you. If society makes sense. Of if you believe in God and Jesus. Then you would have words to help you talk to lost black children about living in the world.

But why did I keep going to gray concrete if it made me feel so bad? If it was so hard? You must be wondering. I was going so I would have money and wouldn't have to live on the street. I was going because as long as I followed some routine in the normal world, I could keep from blowing away, like a tissue in a strong wind. And this world was familiar, or at least there were familiar things about it. And besides, everything wasn't always bad. There were lots of good moments. Tender moments. Precious days with my students. So I was going because I wanted to help people, especially black children, and this was the only thing I knew how to do.

So after I was a substitute, I was a regular teacher with my own classroom. I was at Golden Gate Elementary, teaching sixth grade. That's where you would have found me, five days a week, for over six years. Most of the children there were black. Some were Southeast Asian. Only a few were white. The gray concrete building was like the prison that the refugees on *The Walking Dead* holed up in for a while. Like them, we had a sense of being a family. The gray concrete kept the children safe for a few hours of daylight. The drugs and crime, the horror and pain of the outside world, would be pushing against the tall chain link fence all day. Day in and day out, it would be trying to come crashing in.

Because the rules didn't seem to apply, I would be breaking them, left and right. Just like everyone else. The principal and some of the other teachers seemed like they were living in a make-believe world. The principal, a black woman from Louisiana, would be pretending we were normal people doing normal things, when everyone knew we were not. The school board would be pretending that all things were equal. That the schools in poor neighborhoods and schools in rich neighborhoods were just alike. Then the teachers would be pretending to pretend, so the principal wouldn't bother them. So I would make my own rules. I would teach my students to write, and read, and do math. But not with the books they gave me. And not on the district's schedule. The principal would stand outside my door a lot of the time, listening and looking in. And then she would "write me up" for being insubordinate.

And I would learn to wear my professional man blackness like it was who I was. Like it was me, although it wasn't. I would be trying as best I could to be the black man role model. I could tell that's what the principal and other teachers wanted. They wanted to feel good and proud having a decent black man around. I would try to deepen my voice. To wear the habit of black man-ness. But I'm not so sure that I fooled anyone. Some days I would stand beside my desk and feel my mask running down my face like wet watercolors. I would start stimming, rapidly curling my fingers, and not be able to stop. Some days Ruby would come out and just sit there, listening to the buzzing of florescent lights, not hearing a word the children said.

Sometimes I would yell. Sometimes I would learn to "cap" and "play the dozens" with my children, a language they were speaking to each other all the time, jostling each other in words, back and forth. And every day I would have a hard time making it to the end of the day. After lunch, I would start shaking and want to fall asleep. So I would have to stay on my feet and walk around the classroom the whole time to stay awake. Or take my class outside to the playground, even if it wasn't time for recess. Or play lively games with the class that helped to teach them spelling or things about math. Sometimes I would be a better teacher because I had to try extra hard just to stay present and awake.

Every day, after all of the students were gone, I would stand in the middle of the classroom and close my eyes. I would take a deep breath and exhale for a long time. Sometimes I wanted to cry, but there was no time for crying. I would stand there and become a giant butterfly. Me in my red sannyasin shirt and pants. Me and my beads and mala. Me with my giant red wings. I would feel my soft wings unfolding and touching against the hard walls, the hard desks and chairs. Jeremiah, Lizzy, and Beulah would be holding on to me. I would feel my wings trying to put the color back into things. To brighten them. And each day I would feel myself getting heavier, getting further and further away from being able to lift off.

Sometimes I would be going to gray concrete to sit at a desk and listen to professors. Sometimes I would take a bus to get there. Like when I lived in Berkeley. I would wait for the temperature of the sunlight to be just warm enough before I walked to the bus stop. Other times, I would walk to get to the gray concrete. I would follow the streets and sidewalks with the right light and shadows at the right time of day. I followed the quiet paths, behind someone's garden or yard, beside a blue building. Beside a cedar fence. Beside a green mural. Behind a balcony with an old white porcelain milk canister. In front of a yellow house. Along a brick walkway. I would come through groves of trees where squirrels played and spirits danced in shade. They would be putting their breaths in me. Playing with my skin. Beside a stretch of green grass and onto a concrete sidewalk on campus.

Sometimes I would be running late. And I would have to go down streets bustling with people and quiet noise. Streets where nobody yelled and horns seldom blew. Car engines hummed and the metal beneath their hoods slowly grinded. Sparrows followed me, chirping. I would follow a girl who always wore red rain boots, and a yellow vinyl rain jacket, and carried a children's lunchbox, although she was a college student. She would turn, though, and go into another building, and I would have to walk the rest of the way all alone. She would remind me of sunshine in the yard back in elementary school.

At Berkeley, I was such a famous student, famous to myself. Famous to the desks and chairs and tables and lights and walls. When I sat for hours in empty classrooms and lecture halls, they almost smiled. When I sat in library cubbies or on quiet stone stairways after the building shut down, locked, and everyone had gone home. They almost missed me and Jeremiah and Lizzy on holidays and summer breaks when we weren't around. I liked being a student, at times. I liked talking to quiet people. I liked seeing all of the other people coming and going.

I liked having teachers and learning new things. I had the greatest teachers everywhere I went, not just in classrooms. Famous teachers. Philosophers and mystics, scholars and poets. I met teachers on the way to school and on my way back home. I met them at the back of the bus and on the street corners, in stores and restaurants. I met them at bus and train stations, in homeless shelters, in the lobbies of fancy hotels and halls. I met them under trees in the park, in gardens, in beds of linen and cotton and flannel and down. I must have been doing something good in another life to have such great teachers in this one. All my teachers nurtured and took care of me as if my mama and granny had called them up and said, "Can you please look after our child?" They passed me invisible things. They helped me to keep my dignity.

But once in a while, I got tired of feeling like I could only survive if I was in gray concrete. It was like living my life in a biosphere. That's what I loved about it, but at the same time, that's what made me want to get out. So I would try to escape, but not like someone wanting to escape from prison. But instead, like someone looking in the mirror and thinking about their mama and daddy and whispering, "Please don't let me be like them." I was looking in the mirror when I first came to California. I was hoping I could live a regular life.

I would take the train across the Bay every morning to do carpentry on a job in Berkeley. I liked making things, and I was good at it. I could see angles and how things should fit together. I could make small measurements without a tape measure. Carpentry was one of my birthrights. It was handed down for centuries among slaves on our plantation. The way I learned to cook by holding on to Mama's apron, I learned to do carpentry by watching Daddy from a close distance. I liked the way I disappeared but there I was still, when I worked with my hands. It was relaxing. I didn't just enjoy making things myself, though. I also loved watching others. I could spend the whole day watching construction. It was like being hypnotized. Watching bulldozers and dump trucks. Watching tall cranes rotating slowly and lifting pieces of brick or metal. Watching the patterns the men made, moving about. Tasting the rich scent of opened-up earth. Tasting the scents of hot and cold metal. Tasting the flavor of bricks and all the shades of wood.

For a while, I was feeling so good about escaping. I was feeling so excited about being in a different kind of place. But one day I got lost in pine scent and stepped off a scaffold, falling two stories down. I can still feel the weight of my body, crashing. For eight weeks after that, I was nursing broken bones. I was spending days watching the whites of seagulls against the green grass of the marina. Just like that, my escape was over. I had flown into the sky and fallen hard back to earth.

Then I would start taking the same train I used to take to work, but this time to a gray concrete building at Berkeley, called Lowie Hall. It was the home of the Lowie Museum of Anthropology, and it was like something out of a horror movie, the cheap kind, where the spirit of a murdered tribe comes back seeking revenge for their genocide. It was packed with stolen objects from people across the globe. First Nations, Africans, Pacific Islanders, Indians, and Japanese. Some objects were behind glass in display cabinets so people could look at them. But thousands more were in boxes and crates somewhere in the basement storage. I never wanted to be in the building after dark. It was too full of longings. The shadows started to mourn and move about.

I liked my classrooms, though. They had windows that opened outward on an angle. You just pushed down on them at the top, and they swung open with a creak. At first, I would sit near the window, with my tongue out, panting like a dog in a car, when the car moves out of the city and into the country. My first class was with a famous scholar, who was a funny man, but he wasn't trying to be funny. He smoked a pipe like he was back in an English country house, or standing beside a group of Africans in an anthropology photograph. He was trying to prove that black people had a culture. I know. I couldn't believe it either. In 1978!

I would often lose myself exploring random gray concrete at Berkeley. I had favorites, like the main library. Being in there was like being in an ancient temple. So many men and women had put their minds into it. The design. The patterns. The materials. The angles. So many fingers had put it together, shaped it, planed it, polished it, hammered on it. The stones held so many drops of sweat. The high rotunda-like ceilings drew my breath upward; the space and light drew my body, making it taller.

I got lost in the dark alleys of "the stacks" and in the subterranean and attic cubbies where bits of light filtered in through low-lying clouds. It was so quiet. Gothic. All of the metal shelves and cages. The thick, painted concrete floors and flickering fluorescent lights. The sheer weight of it in my mind almost gave me a hernia. Now and then, a clanking sound echoed through the dimly lit, gray space. It was like being on a spaceship in a science-fiction movie. Moving through space. Listening to the soothing, low bass drone of the engine. Everyone I passed was so focused on their papers or their books; I was like a wind they didn't notice. I walked along the long hallways, around stacks of shelves, trying not to laugh out loud. I lost days and weeks pulling books about folklore and anthropology, art and photography, off metal shelves and thumbing through them, drinking words and photographs.

At times, I perched at a window so that I could look out at all the people, all the characters. So I could have my cake and eat it. Looking out was one of my favorite things. I thought that I was whatever I saw. That all those other worlds were me. I could watch me until nothing else existed.

I didn't know it then, but being in gray concrete at UC Berkeley was one of the highlights of my life. I was feeling like I had security. "Security" meant not having too many things to think about or to do. It meant having everything done at the end of the day, and no anxiety, and no guilt. It meant not having to worry about money. Having people helping me, and having a place to live with a nice bed. Having the perfect routine, a routine like a room with the perfect light, and a window opened just the right amount, with just the right amount of breeze, of green leaves and sunlight, at just the right temperature.

When I was in gray concrete at Berkeley, I was often relaxed. I was writing poetry. I was meeting people, and having friends, and trying to have relationships. There were days when my mind didn't show up, and I would stay home and cover myself with blankets and pillows. Most days were a series of small disasters, as far as my body went. As far as being overwhelmed by sunlight and noise, and something, somewhere aching. But that was my life. Most days were pretty good. Now and then I went out. I sometimes went to movies at the Pacific Film Archives. I went to museums and symphonies, concerts and plays.

I sometimes wandered into receptions at art galleries and stood in the corner and sipped a glass of wine, even though I didn't like drinking. There would often be black spirits trapped in white spaces at events like those. They would be in the music. They would be in the uppermost corners or floating through the crowd, turned down low, but I could still hear them screaming. Blues. Jazz. White people couldn't live without them, but they would never say "please" to the spirits. They would just say, "OK. Play. Sing. Sing good like you know you can do."

Sometimes while I was looking at a painting, my hand would start stimming, and someone would come up to me and smile and start talking, because they thought I was a famous artist, or an art dealer, or a critic. Or because they thought I looked interesting and mysterious. I enjoyed those conversations. The person would be smart and subtle. They would be like an amazing meal, in a quiet restaurant, with golden low light, at a table near a large front window, with a breeze coming in the door whenever someone came and went. But when the person turned to talk to someone else, or to get another glass of wine, I breathed in deeply, filling myself with their flavor, with the flavors of the entire gallery, and with the taste on the cool air against my face as I slipped out.

The worst gray concrete was when I was a student at UCLA. I was taking the bus from Culver City, and Venice, to Westwood. I was talking to palm trees at the bus stop and asking them to shelter my eyes and throat from the burning of smog. I was having one of the hardest times in my life. I knew I was in trouble the minute I got to Los Angeles. I couldn't find the city. It was too spread out. When I first got there, I wrote on a napkin: *There is rubble and ash beneath glitter and streets too wide to cross before the light turns. There is no earth, no green, no softness. Everything is too far, and the brightness of sun off metal and glass is blinding. There are too few trees to filter the light, and so some of it ricochets off the ocean of glass, cars, and rooftops, rises and explodes over the city like a nuclear bomb.*

I was working hard to function at UCLA. The campus had as much gray concrete as a small city. Each day I was stranded there. I would hurry up and get to the building where the folklore program was. I would hurry up to get out of the brightness, out of the noise of so many other students, of sirens and engines. I would be listening, but I would never hear any birds. I would be watching and listening for quiet places, but I never found any. I would be going to the folklore building, "the bunker," as I called it, but inside, florescent lights buzzed and flickered and the small spaces of offices and classrooms were packed with other people. Each day, I was just waiting until it was over and I could go home.

When I was in the gray concrete of UCLA, I didn't realize it was so prestigious. I was being practical by going there. I was doing what I knew how to do to stay safe and function. I wanted to keep studying folklore, and they had a folklore program. I wanted to have time to keep writing poetry and get published. I wanted to stay in California. And I wanted to make my granny famous by writing about her. But I knew nothing about university rankings. I knew nothing about conferences, networking, or academic professions. I had no sense of the value of a PhD or the difference it made what university it came from. I had no sense of how it might be related to the future. There was no future in my mind. I was like my favorite cartoon character, Mr. Magoo. I was driving my car across a moving steel girder, way up in the air, oblivious to the danger. I was going nowhere in particular, trying to be happy.

All the Green and Blue

Turquoise, or amber?
Light, or bending matter?

"Just be like a white ox in a green field," the Zen masters say. "Don't let anything move you." But everything was always moving me. Every temperature. Every tone. Every color. Every shade. Especially outdoors. My favorite spaces weren't yellow houses or gray concrete. They were the green and blue of outdoors. I couldn't live without those colors. They were like touchstones. I could relax my eyes and not see the outlines of things, just the colors, and I would be at home and be happy. When it was perfect, outdoors was where I inhaled and exhaled the best. The problem was, there was almost never any perfection.

Outdoors was full of dangers. First was just the dizziness of walking out of a door, any door, out of spaces with shape and size into the shapeless, out of timid lighting into brightness. But the danger was the other side of what I loved so much. There was no time outdoors. Nothing to lean on. I could never comprehend the fields of objects and light, the mysterious and hypnotic fields of proximity and distance that put me into trance. Words disappeared into those fields, did not exist. Temperatures were the bodies of water that floated other bodies, but temperatures were always "almost," never truly safe, never "all the time" or even for a certain reliable time like an object in a room. Temperatures were layers of currents that could burn one part of me and at the same time chill another. Outdoors, I knew where I was in the universe, but I didn't know where I was on earth.

The thing people call "nature" was a danger. I call it the raw earth, the raw universe, the harsh laws of the planet. In Virginia, it meant asthma attacks; the earth attacked my breath. It attacked with insect bites, pollen, mold, dust, animal hair and fur. It attacked with light that was too bright and temperatures that threw my balance off. With cold, and shadows that turned the solid matter of my body into perforated liquid and vapor seeking shelter in the wind and clouds. Nature was a seesaw of a moon pulling tides inside me from side to side, and it was the invisible forces between the moon and the water.

And then the city was a danger along with the other dangers, and it was a danger in itself. The barrage of city noise and other senses. In the city, I became a sense. I became the drunken man at the party, the one with clothes on at the orgy, the blind beggar on the street, the lost dog walking against the current and dodging traffic and people's feet. The city was too small and too large, all together, changing nature, simulating anchored matter, at once below the everlasting blue of skies and splotched with patterns of green.

But the dangers in California were different from those in Virginia. The light was a different hue. The temperatures of the sun and the wind were different. The tones of the green were lighter. In Virginia, sometimes a bird would burst into something like fury in the sunlight and turn almost white. But it was darkness the forest was mainly after. In California, birds carried light across the sky like redemption songs, like echoes of reeds, vibrating in the treble.

In Virginia, the trees could hardly wait to touch. To close the paths of sunlight so that everything was bathed in shade. The shade was cool. It moved like waves. It radiated like the heat from a pot-bellied iron stove or from a steam radiator. In California, the trees kept their distances, leaving the sky to open us up, as if we had no limit, as if we belonged to lightness, like marrow belongs to bones. In California, Ruby's heart beat like a sparrow. I inhaled as deeply as I could, and inside my lungs was nothing but clarity. I laid my burdens down. I was baptized in redwood mist and born again in green firs and eucalyptuses.

My girlfriend, Virginia, bought a white Volkswagen Rabbit, and she drove all the time. I was so happy sitting in the passenger seat. I could look at things in the city. I could look at the yellow and white lines on the roads to see if they were irregular or perfectly straight. I could look at the shapes of tall buildings and measure their angles. I could feel their textures. I rolled around in white adobe like a hippo in a watering hole. I spread my skin around steel and brick and concrete, iron rails and wood. I was mesmerized by the architecture. The shapes and colors of houses were so lively. Their faces had so many little sections, ornaments and designs. Each part was often painted a different shade or color. I could wave my wand at things that were out of place and fix them. Like windows that weren't perfectly symmetrical, or corners that weren't exactly forty-five degrees.

I could look at the people. There were so many people doing things outdoors all of the time, in a way I had never seen! The colors and scents of people blended with those of houses and roads, of sidewalks and parks and streets. It was the seventies and eighties, and it was like everyone walked in the same spirit. I could feel it in the Castro or the Mission, Noe Valley, the Fillmore, J-Town or North Beach, Bayview or the Tenderloin, Duboce or the length of Haight. The people were the city. Their bodies were in so many sizes and shapes, and they emitted so many different colors. They dressed themselves in colors, shapes, and textures that were new to me. The asymmetry of clothes sometimes made the streets tilt and the trolley tracks scream. Spirits twirled around light poles like children around maypoles. It was like a carnival all the time. Thousands of spirits were walking among the people. Some of them were smiling because they were so happy. Some of them looked somberly out from restaurant windows at people on the streets. It was the first time I had ever seen a jealous spirit.

There were many clusters of green in the city, magic places with their own neighborhoods of spirits. One was Golden Gate Park, a giant stretch of green, over one thousand acres and thousands of species of plants. It had forests and meadows, groves and gardens, and alcoves of shadows and lights. The trees I loved most were the palms, eucalyptuses, and gingkoes. I loved that they had room to spread their branches and how so much light could touch the ground beneath them. Their shadows held me like I was a shadow, like Uncle T and the other old people where I grew up held me. Sometimes I would happen upon spirits while walking on paths through branches and bushes with Jeremiah and Lizzy. They would hover like clouds. I think sometimes when people die, their spirits move into seeds. Sometimes they move into the light and shadows beneath trees. Sometimes they start rising and run into the canopy of leaves, and feel like they're in heaven, and just stay there.

Then there were the palm trees lining Delores Avenue. The sunlight of spirits flooding the Mission District, dancing off the skins of peppers, plantains, avocados, and lemons on tables along the sidewalks. Other spirits sang in the bougainvillea and washed over our bodies, spewing from the white blossoms of night jasmine along the avenues. Others came alive in the currents of light bulbs, in the multicolored neon and filaments pulsing and holding steady and humming for distances as far as the eye could see. When they saw that I could see them, their colors deepened.

In California I learned to ride buses and trains, streetcars and trolleys, looking out of windows. Somedays, when I was going somewhere, like looking for a job, I walked and walked, tasting scents and spirits in green places. When I lived in Berkeley, I used to walk and look at rooftops. There were some made of red clay tiles on some buildings that hypnotized me. They were like half circles. There were so many different patterns in the tiles, depending on where I stood, or how I turned my head, or how I squinted my eyes. Turning one way, I saw waterfalls. Turning another way, I saw a rippled street, climbing into the hills. Turning another way, I saw the top halves of cups or glasses, turned on the side and stacked and lined up in rows, longing for their other halves like slaves longing for freedom.

I was watching so many people, so many faces and bodies carrying different stories like *Little Red Riding Hood* or *A Tisket a Tasket* carrying baskets to their mamas. I was trying to read each story, without staring, without being noticed. I was walking through downtown Berkeley, and then through Sproul Plaza on the Berkeley campus. Sometimes there were speakers talking about political and social things, and musicians playing flutes and guitars, and people handing out pamphlets. All of the white light bouncing off the surfaces of white skin made me dizzy. Girls were like sparklers on the Fourth of July, as many colors of light exploded from their elbows and shoulders, shoulder blades, knees, and backs of the knees—in ripples—ear lobes, chins, teeth, necks, foreheads, ankles, thighs, toes, fingers, hair, and exposed buttocks. I liked something I got from the people, but I wished I could be invisible and drink it, and taste it, and study it. I had a hunger for it. Sex was a little like that. The other person's desire gave me desire. The desires of nature, of life, were also like that. The flight of pods and urgency of seeds burying into earth gave me flight.

There were two men on Telegraph Avenue I always remember. One of them wore a paper bag on his head with cutouts for his eyes. He walked with his hand up to his face, as if the light was overwhelming. He wore a suit, though, and I wondered if he was going to a job. If he was going to a job, did he take his paper bag off once he got there? There was another man who stumbled along with a folder of papers up to his face. He looked sideways as he walked, making sure that no one's glance could touch him and set his face on fire.

Down Telegraph was a spirit city I reveled in. Sometimes I saw the field that had been there before the city came, with apple trees. Sometimes I stepped on ancient grass instead of walking on concrete. Trees on either side of the street talked to each other, and their leaves kept trying to reach across the slowly moving traffic below them and embrace. They were like Romeo and Juliet, except, because they could never touch, they would always have each other.

The spirits under the trees became some of my best friends. They were so old and moved so slowly. One of them was named Javed. Jeremiah saw him first, and called his name, and they hugged in a shadow and light cave beneath the tree outside a sushi restaurant. I walked into the cave as if I was coming home, as if I was walking into a palace. Javed was the gold of mangoes where the green begins to turn red. He had a white beard, and he moved as if moving didn't matter, a blur, as if however slowly he turned or raised his hand, his body was always a half beat behind some other body. I hugged Javed, and for a while I couldn't stop myself from crying.

Vendors lined the streets, and some of them were talking with the spirits. They were selling incense, candles, jewelry, Rasta hats and hippie hats, pants and shirts and skirts, buttons, CDs and cassette tapes, oils and essences, art they had painted or cooked in kilns or carved from wood or stone or soldered with metal. They sold posters; stickers; postcards; ethnic instruments; herbs; teas; Guatemalan, Indian, and Chinese blankets and fabrics. They sold African prints and a thousand different pipes and bowls and bongs.

When I was walking through Berkeley, I didn't feel much danger. It was too small to get lost in. I learned how much outdoors I could take before I lost my focus, and I was sure to get home before I melted down. I learned how much of each street and each cluster of green I could take in what amount of time. And usually, there wasn't any hurry. I wasn't trying to get somewhere on time, and so if I lost time or direction for a while, it didn't usually matter.

Virginia also loved the blue and green. She loved being in nature and camping and hiking. But going camping, I did feel danger. It's not something most black people would want to be doing. First of all, it's a luxury. But second, once you leave the city, anything can happen. It doesn't matter what state you're in if it's still in America. A lot of racists live out of the city, even in California. Skinheads, KKK members, survivalists. That's why on the West Coast black people say, "If you want to stay alive, stay on the I-5." That's why when I went camping I never saw another black person. In the city, you have some safety; you have communities and numbers. But once you leave that behind, you're in the wilderness on your own, and a black man with a white woman in the jungle outside the city might never be heard from again.

But I was usually glad once we got where we were going. The wilderness was welcoming. The redwoods were like some people on the spectrum; they didn't want to be touched. But I couldn't always help myself. I couldn't always keep from leaning in against them and pressing my nose into their scents. From looking up into branches that seemed to rise for miles. From falling in love. We hiked in mountains, in valleys and meadows, through forests. We camped in more places than I can remember, like Mono Lake, Point Reyes, Tahoe, Mendocino, Jenner, Big Basin, Sequoia, and Sierra Nevada. I sometimes took my guitar, a book, and my writing pad. Virginia, and friends we went with, would be setting up the tent, and cooking, and sometimes going on walks. I would be sitting nearby, playing my guitar, or writing, or reading. I could feel Virginia so deeply when she was putting up the tent and getting things ready. She turned the color of purple irises in the filtered light of the trees. Our turning greener than firs, together, in the secluded green light of our campsite, before the orange crackling of fire, was one of our deepest bonds. In those moments, I felt like I was out of danger.

Before anything and after everything else, for me, was the ocean. The Pacific. Standing beside it, I exhaled for days. My past began to come out of me in waves that disappeared into the currents. When I floated across the ocean, I knew what it would feel like to be on my home planet. There would be nothing but blue, the slightest motion, and distance. There would be knowing that no time had really passed and nothing had really happened. I loved the sound of waves sloshing inward, the seagulls and the drifting sailboats, the ships passing slowly in the fog. I loved what the ocean did to time. It slowed time down, suspended it. I liked the way the kelp smelled, but I didn't like the sand. I didn't like walking on it or touching it, and I didn't like the dampness beneath it that tried to tear into my body. If I had to walk across a desert on grass, I could probably make it. But if I had to walk across one on sand, I would throw my arms up and say, "Please, just go ahead now and take me."

When I was near the ocean, I forgot all dangers, and that was part of the problem.

When I was in Los Angeles, I hungered for the green and blue. But the palms and placid yards beneath the smog-tinted sky were not enough. So I snuck out to be in more, to be in nothing but the wildest blue. I was being like a roommate I had in college who had bipolar disorder. Sometimes she would rebel and not take her meds. She wanted to feel free, normal. But she would slowly become like someone wild. Once we had to hold her down while she was screaming. There were times like that for me at UCLA. I would want to be normal and do things other people did and have fun.

My favorite place to go looking for greens and blues was Venice Beach. Like Telegraph, in Berkeley, it was a carnival, except a much bigger one and at the beach. I fit in at carnivals, along with all the other misfits, along with all the other delicate people with spirits of wonder, the special ones that "normal" people call "weirdoes" or "freaks." Like people in the film *The King of Hearts.*

But when I got off the bus at Venice Beach, there were so many scents. There were so many textures, sounds, and tastes that I was dripping them as I walked. My pores were getting showered. Getting bathed. I became dripping, of burnt garlic and lemon. Of grilled chicken skins in black pepper. Of green peppers, parsley, and cilantro. Of ginger, turmeric, and cumin. Kielbasa and ketchup. Seaweed and crabs. Hotdogs and burgers. Of a thousand body scents. Of ylang-ylang oil and frankincense, myrrh, rose, and amber lotions, shampoos, detergents, incenses, and sweat.

I was hypnotized watching skaters dance to "Girls Just Wanna Have Fun." In a large holy circle of wind, dancing to the spirits while the bass pounded through huge boom boxes, shuffling my bones. I watched jugglers tossing knives and chainsaws and black acrobats leaping into pyramids, into pinwheels spinning. I watched a magic woman with a table of tricks, and two black men strumming Stevie Wonder so sweetly I almost cried. And I watched swimsuit models posing in front of bikini shops; me and Jeremiah and Lizzy, laughing, as everything we saw was taken by the wind and ocean mist into some alternate reality.

And I was mesmerized watching the barely clothed bodies. I longed to see the patterns they made with other bodies. The tattoos and dimples, scars and bone angles, arcs of movement and pimples. The flowing currents of cellulite. The cabinets of muscles and fat. A brightly colored, moving masterpiece on a canvas of light. Now and then, someone would say to me, out of the blue, "How do you like my body?" They would stop as they were passing and put their hands on their hips and smile. Or they would turn the other way and look back over their shoulders and let their backbones slip like they were going to break. They would smile at my embarrassment as I retreated into the shade under trees and turned into a spirit.

The rules of Venice seemed to be: Show as much of your body as you can. Talk with your body. Sing with your body. Make your body a song. Make your body a story. Cry with your body. Plead with your body. Get your joy with your body. Sometimes I felt that the songs and cries of bodies were so desperate it must be near the end of time. Other times I thought, *This is the way we should be talking; this is a more honest conversation; this is more real.*

Some days I took my camera to the beach and photographed the special places where the spirits lived, where the shadows were mysteriously hinged to light. Some of the stairways had textures that came alive in certain light and their shadows became their own entities, their own vessels, hovering like clouds, rippling like sheets on a clothesline in strong wind. Some of the rounded cement tables had shadows that played music while the spirits danced. There was a vendor's table with pretty bottles where the spirits liked to blow over the lips of the bottles and make them sing. On the days that I took my camera, I tried to be invisible. I would not even look at people, except in mirrors. Many of the vendors along the boardwalk had mirrors at their tables, so that people could see themselves when they tried on a hat, necklace, or whatever. I would watch people only in those mirrors. Cameras drew people, though. Many people wanted their picture taken. They dreamed of being discovered, of getting their break in the movies, in modeling, or on television. They would think I might be somebody important, and even if I wasn't, they would pose and plead, "Please take my picture."

I would sit on bleachers and watch the bodybuilders in a giant, fenced-in space along the boardwalk. Some of their bodies were oiled and glistened like glass in the sun, and they liked showing off their hardened shoulders and abs, tight thighs and buttocks. They grunted like they were having sex when they lifted the weights. They sighed like they were having orgasms when they sat the weights down. Some of the people in the bleachers seemed to be having orgasms too.

Near the weightlifting cages were the basketball hoops. That's where men went to proclaim they were men. They went there and took their shirts off and walked around like roosters. White girls went there to proclaim they liked men. They especially liked black men. They liked their bodies and their rhythm. They liked their talk. They liked the contradictions between white and black bodies, between the frightening power of muscular black men in the flesh and their feeble power in society or their vulnerability next to their white skin.

Men and boys went there to proclaim they liked men, for different reasons. Some liked to imagine they *were* the guys playing basketball or lifting weights. Some liked looking simply because, through their eyes, men were the prettiest things. I liked to watch all the people. Those playing and those watching, as if the carnival was just mine. As if it belonged to me. I drank it, and no one could stop me. I took my skin off and basked in it. The tender tissue beneath my skin was dripping. I became the alien in their midst. I inhaled the light. I inhaled even more deeply at times when I felt the familiar anxiety that there was something so wrong with me. That I had no right to happiness. I inhaled as if I was draining smoke from a giant bong when I felt the familiar guilt that I was simply fooling other people, pretending to be one of them.

At times, even in my seminars, I was still at the beach. I rubbed the beach on myself, like animals rub on layers of mud. Like ancient hunters rubbed themselves with the grease of their kill. I rubbed it on to protect me from the din of cars and buses. From the vastness and strangeness of the campus. From the glares and slights and dismissals of the educated people. From the thing and time and place they called the normal. From the brutality of the thing they called the civilized. Inside the city of Venice was a second city of my tribe. Even if I rarely talked to them. The homeless. The people in wheelchairs with their garbage bags and voodoo-painted carts filled with their things and their brightly painted bicycles. The artists and musicians. I could tell them by the bronze glow they gave off. I could tell them by the way their colors opened up and took me in. I could tell them by the songs their silences played on the pores of my body. Among them, I was at home.

When I would leave Venice Beach I would walk to the bus stop, and I would get on the bus, and I would be tingling with current. I would be spastic in my bus seat. I would get home and my body would be a storm of trembling, of lightning and thunder. Sometimes it went on for days. I would carefully order all the sights I had seen at the beach, in my mind. The colors, the shapes, the scents I had gathered. The glances into my spirit. The words I heard passing from members of my tribe. "Yeah, beautiful." "Yeah, brother." "Yeah, umm humh." I would order them as neatly as glasses and cups in a kitchen cabinet. Then I would open the cabinet and smile, and close it, and do the same thing again. On those days, I would not talk. After days of trembling, of my skin crackling like a loose electric wire, torrents of rain would pummel the ground inside me. And after the storm had passed, I would feel an incredible peace. It would grip me like the tightening hand of a dying person holding on to my wrist.

There were days I had trouble getting home from the beach. There were times when my mind spun around like the rainbow-colored Mac apple spins when the system is overloaded. I would get caught in a loop and then couldn't get out of it. I might be at the bus stop coming back from the beach. Or at a bus stop on a wide, busy street that suddenly seemed unfamiliar. I might be passing a group of trees or cluster of green shrubs when shadows moved independently out of them. The traffic would sometimes take my mind. Especially at noon, when the sun was too bright, or when I misjudged the time and it got dark before I left the beach. Some days I just couldn't leave, even when I knew I should.

I had to see the sunset. To hear the way the waves sounded, splashing against the sand when the colors of the sun were softly breaking the west sky apart. The way silhouettes came out of hiding. Silhouettes of palm trees and buildings. Silhouettes of people walking across strips of grass or sidewalks or sand. I had to taste the air when the tourists were starting to leave and my tribe started being more themselves. When the tastes of comfort and danger mixing on my tongue almost gave me goosebumps. I had to find the patterns in the sounds of the waves. I had to see how the blue left the ocean at sundown, to see if I could discover where it went. I had to speak to the seagulls one last time before leaving. I had to keep an eye on the people in the wheelchairs, and the children who were by themselves, so that no one would harm them. How could I leave when so many things needed me?

But everything changed in the dark, with all the neon-colored signs and jarring headlights. Distances changed and became hard to gauge. Directions lost any meanings they might have had. Time completely disappeared. The day city moved aside, like in the movie *Dark City*. Another city took its place. Blue disappeared and everything turned black. I could see buildings in the distance, like in a dream, rearranging themselves. Sometimes I would sit on a bench at a bus stop on an unfamiliar street, and I would forget absolutely everything. For a while, I would be all right. But eventually, I would get so lonely sitting there, but I wouldn't know that I was lonely. I would be like a numbed tooth, screaming. The rule was never to get on a bus if I wasn't sure where it was going. What was the right street? What was the right number for my bus? Where was the arched building that was supposed to be at the right bus stop? At times, things came back into clarity after a little while. Then I could think about where I needed to go to catch the bus home. Other times, no clarity came, and I would just keep sitting. I remembered that if I didn't move, I couldn't get more lost.

Once, a deaf African man sat beside me on the bench. He showed me his notebooks filled with poems and dazzling otherworldly watercolors. They were so beautiful! He would paint the pages first and then write words here and there, over the paintings. He wrote words like Ashanti, heart, rise, red, dye, and magnificent. He gestured to me to come with him, and reluctantly I did. By then, the traffic had died down and the buses were hardly running. He took me to his home, which was a cardboard box. I was sad and anxious that I couldn't be at my house, and sleep in my own bed, and touch my own things. The man had dirty fingernails, but he didn't smell bad. He smelled like cookies and dirt and lard, and his scent reminded me of Uncle T. The way people smell when they live close to the ground and they don't change their clothes for a long time.

His box had a broken radio in it. A broken piece of mirror and a red beer can with a picture of an almost naked woman. A pair of tattered biking gloves. Next to his box was a big refrigerator box where two white boys about thirteen slept. But they didn't seem white. They talked more like black people in the city than I did. I don't know what the homeless people saw when they looked at me, but they gave me water and crackers. They warned me to be careful that no one stole my wallet.

On the other side of the African man, in a smaller box, was a girl about nineteen. She had a penis, but that was the only boy thing about her. I liked her because she wasn't dressed up and her short hair and soft cheeks were so pretty, and something about her was calm and steady, and she looked at me without her eyes. She made me smile and fell asleep with me, and she smelled like cherry chewing gum and motor grease. I held on to her like I held on to the handles of a Ferris wheel once, when it started climbing, desperate and terrified. The next morning, when the noise of the nearby traffic woke me up, the girl was gone. The African man was gone. The two white boys were gone. The fire had gone out in the big trashcan, and I was alone in the cardboard village beneath the underpass.

Professor in the Silver Town

When in Rome...

Snow fell. In the city of autumn brown light, where sat the silver town. Silver light, like a spoon. Silver, like an aluminum cup. Silver, like a nickel. Silver, like a shiny buckle. Snow fell. I hadn't seen snow in over ten years. On postcards. In movies. But not in the real world. It reminded me of days in childhood. It reminded me of my sisters and my brothers, throwing snowballs and coming in to the warmth of the potbellied stove and mama yelling to get out of those wet things and don't track that mud and water across her floor. My sisters and my brothers are in my skin. Diffused through pores and corpuscles. They are like melanin, like rhythm. Like tones, like a tune. They are the flesh of my flesh.

Snow fell, and I was sitting there, watching, as dazed as an alien who had come through a time portal. Like a swami who had fallen back to earth from the fifth heaven. I was like someone in a movie who had been beamed to a strange planet, but the transporter malfunctioned and only a part of me made it. Part of me was still somewhere in between, a trail of vapor stretching across Utah, Texas, California, and Arizona. I had landed in a bare room, in a house with no furniture and no heat, and through a fog, I could see the devil standing in the corner. I could feel his breath. He was holding pictures in an outstretched hand, a safe life with a car, a house, awards, honors, books, and health insurance. The picture I cared the most about was me sitting around a Christmas tree with my son, opening presents, but to get that I had to take the whole package. Me and the devil had met before, and made bargains. We had made them quick, before the spirits and the angels came and turned the room light. This time it took me all of five minutes to say yes, and I would have said yes even if I hadn't been in a daze. I needed so badly to feel human. To stop feeling like a rabbit, running and hiding, panting, hyperventilating and out of breath.

Snow clung to the branches and bent them over like a lover bending over a lover. It bent the thin limbs of saplings or scrubs, berry bushes and thorned tentacles of roses down to the rising river of snow, like a preacher leaning bodies back into the holy water; like John, dipping Jesus. Snow fell, and with it, quiet. At last, the quiet. Where do the birds go, when snow is falling, I wondered, where do they go? Are there secret tunnels of sanctuary, spun from the lightness of flight, somewhere among the trees? Snow fell, and I had no coat. I had no boots or gloves either, and this was biting cold that took no prisoners.

I hadn't had time to really think about what coming eastward meant, or what it meant to become a professor. I tried hard to grasp the reality of it, but it was like catching smoke with my fingers. I couldn't move from the window, looking out, and flashing back, two years, five years, one year. I was back at the window in my Oakland apartment, with my son, Nick, who was then only four. I was wondering how we were going to make it. I was watching the repo man taking the van, and trying not to let Nick know that anything was happening. I was thinking about the sentences his mother was famous for: "You'll never amount to anything," and "I won't let you see him." I was thinking about all of the friends and the money I had lost, because I didn't know anything about lawyers or court. I was hearing her lawyer calling me a deadbeat dad. I was hearing the judge saying, "You niggers are all the same."

I was missing and missing and missing Nick. I talked to him every weekend, but that wasn't the same. I would fly to California twice a year and bring him back, and when he got older, I would buy his tickets and send them to his mother. But sometimes she wouldn't take him to the airport or put him on the plane. And this was one of those times. I was going to have another lonely Christmas, with snow outside, blowing into drifts, and icicles dripping from the roof's edge, as I sat inside, pretending nothing was the matter.

I was so happy whenever he came. When I went to meet his plane, and he walked off last, escorted by the flight attendant, I almost broke into tears. Flying so many miles alone. I wanted to protect him. From everything. It was hard to know that I couldn't. Taking him back to the airport was even harder. I tried to be strong. Hugging him and watching him disappear down the boarding ramp with the attendant. Waiting for the other passengers to board. For the door to close and the plane to slowly drift out onto the runway and lift off. The sight of the plane climbing into the sky turned all of my strength to weakness, and I felt like I was disappearing.

Out the window, I watched a large tree branch sagging more and more under the weight of snow. And then it finally cracked, split and crashed half way across the street. The creaking, cracking and splitting and thumping down were filled with cries of pain, and I was back in downtown San Francisco, a few months earlier, in the middle of the big earthquake. There was a long, low moaning and then things started to sway, when they were supposed to be steady. The buildings shifted their angles and the windows and doors could not stand it. They tried to stay square and rectangular, like soldiers who have been ordered to stay at attention, but they couldn't hold. Glass popped from windows and people came running out of buildings and put their arms out to balance themselves, and held their arms up to keep from getting cut.

Pipes screamed as they were ripped from their sockets, and water spurted out of them like lost dreams. Electric current fled from wires and conduits and danced in the air, going "na na na na na." Traffic lights went out, but everyone saw green anyway, and raced through intersections like lemmings toward cliffs. Tires screeched and metal crashed against other metal. Sirens screamed into reddened air thick with the tastes of smoke, of something burning, of fear and tears and blood. Heels scurried and concrete and plaster buckled, and white powder and debris drifted down around us like snow. I walked in a daze, listening to the broadcast on radios that people who had run shrieking from buildings were listening to as they stood, shaken, along the streets.

Standing at the window, I still had that feeling of not being able to trust the ground beneath my feet. Everything teetered. The illusion of stability was gone, and there was nothing to replace it.

The idea that I could become a "professor" broke slowly, over years. It was a slow breaking, like a wave that starts off the coasts of China, and a year later makes to an American beach. I never wanted a career. I had always thought of my life as my career. Writing poetry. Tasting things. Deciphering colors. Witnessing. I always thought that's why I was put here, that this was my way of making the world better. It had never occurred to me that I'd ever leave the West Coast. My communities and families and friends were there. The ocean was there. The eucalyptuses and redwoods. How could I leave them? I knew I needed a better job, to get more stable, but I thought I'd end up at an alternative college in the Southwest, where there would be lots of art, people of color, and no grades. I thought the universe would take care of it. But the universe is full of surprises and tricks.

Until then, I hadn't fully understood desperation. I knew what the word meant, but I didn't know the feeling. I had seen it plenty of times. The first desperation I saw was in the scent of slave spirits running through the woods where I grew up, trying to escape. I was in bed sick for weeks after feeling their terror. When I was eighteen, I spent three weeks around desperate people. I took a job working for a company that sent young people around the country selling magazine subscriptions door to door. The ad said "Travel! See the country!" That sounded so cool, but it wasn't. They took in mostly teens from inner cities and held them prisoners. They kept us in a hotel and taught us the sales pitches, and took us in vans to New Hampshire, Rhode Island, and Vermont, dropped us off in rich neighborhoods and told us we had to sell or they would leave us out there, or take us and pimp us out. Now and then, the drivers really would leave people, a hundred miles from the hotel.

We were in their debt, until we sold enough to get out, for the hotel, for food, and for whatever else we needed. A few people did all right, because they were used to hustling. But most of us didn't. One guy latched onto me and followed me around, always talking about the house he was going to buy for his mama. When I was sneaking away one night, trying to escape, he followed me for blocks. "But how are we going to buy those houses for our mamas?" he kept saying, over and over. At the time, it didn't make sense. Why didn't he just do what I was doing, and leave? But now, I understood desperation. I understood the feeling.

Little by little, I got the hang of how things worked at the university and what the rules were in my department, in the silver town. They were so different than the rules in other places where I had lived, or even in other universities. They were different because I was in Missouri now, and because I was a professor, rather than a student. There were different rules for professors, but no one had ever told me what they were. I was a non-swimmer thrown into the water. I would learn to swim, or sink trying. If Brer Rabbit could get Brer Fox to throw him in the briar patch; if Shine could swim all the way back to Harlem; if Sweetback could make it to Mexico, I could do this.

The first rule was to always wear a mask. Otherwise, I felt too naked. Too many gazes were crashing against me and I was used to blending in. To hiding in or outside of crowds. There had always been a lot more "different" looking people than me for other people to stare at. I could pass good, as far as how I looked, especially on a college campus. But I was used to being a student on campuses. I could stand among the shrubs and be green, and no one would notice. But professors are paid to stand out, and so they do. They wear different clothes. They look like they're carrying heavy weights, and at any minute, they could topple over. They look like their bodies are there, but their minds are some other place.

At first, I tried wearing a paper mask, but too much got through it. All the things getting through were hurting. Then I tried wearing a silk mask, because it felt so soft against my skin. But that only lasted for a week, and I came home in tears. Then, I tried wearing wood, but it wouldn't bend around my head. Finally, I tried copper, and I knew that was it. The copper talked to me and reminded me of things. "Remember," it would say, "don't try talking about real things in an unreal place." "Don't be blinded by the silver light." "Don't fall asleep and get killed in the quiet jungle."

So, I put on a copper mask and sent myself off to work. The man in the copper mask could talk to people. He could teach and go to meetings. He knew when to smile and when to be witty, because I had taught him. I had picked it up from watching others. It wasn't that hard. In fact, a part of the difficulty was that it wasn't that hard. The man in the copper mask would be talking and I would be listening to colors, thinking about the clouds, the hues of blue skies. I would be lost in a phrase in a song or a hibiscus blossoming in my front garden. But it was not unusual for the man in the copper mask to come home after work, take his mask off, lay his head on my shoulder, and burst into tears.

The second rule was, don't speak everyday talk. Otherwise, people think you're stupid. I had been used to street talk, Rasta talk, sannyasin talk. Therapy talk. I was used to talking as a way of revealing myself, of sharing feelings. But the rule was don't share feelings in the silver town, and use only intellectual words that mimic thought. So I had to put away the words I loved the most, the ones that made me feel that I was beautiful, and whole, and good. I had to put away "cool," or "man," or "brother," or "sister," or "I-rie." I had to put away "mama," "y'all," "baby," and "ain't," "samadhi," and "enlightenment." I had to pick up "theory," "unpack," and "critique," "epistemological," "discourse," and "trope," and put them in my briefcase and folders.

The third rule had to do with the body. I had been used to the languages of dance and touch, to holding someone's hand, and hugging. I loved hugs, as long as no one breathed on my neck. But one day in the silver town, I hugged someone and I could hear people loudly sucking in their breaths, putting their hands over their mouths, and staring downward, as if I was obscene. So the next rule I learned in the silver town was, "never touch anybody." Live in a touchless world. Live alone with skin that is always crying.

Dancing was one of my very favorite things. I used to go to clubs and conjure spirits with my body. With my heart. Sometimes people stared at me and cleared a circle. Sometimes the spirits came out of my body and took over the club. Blue and maroon me and the moon, and all the other repossessed bodies. This was one of my deepest loves. The freedom of it. The beauty! I would never forget when I was young and my body could hardly move. So I never lost the sense that moving was a miracle, or that me getting the hang of it was the biggest miracle of all.

And one day I moved my body, at a faculty party. I kept waiting for the music. For the dancing. Why did they call it a party? People held glasses of wine and sipped every so often, in between saying clever things. So I played music in my mind, and ever so slightly, moved my body. And then I heard someone say something about Japan, and I said that I loved sumo wrestlers because their fat was so sexy. A silence came over the room, as if someone had died. So I learned rules number four and five. Don't dance with my body. Don't hang out with rhythm in public. Rhythm is a criminal here, and will get me sentenced or exiled. The other rule was don't say anything to anyone about sumo wrestlers.

The sixth rule was to be a single gender. Pick a gender and stick with it, preferably, the one your body says you are. I was so terrible to Ruby. I sold her skirts and dresses and packed away her earrings and necklaces. I wouldn't let her walk down any street. I barely let her lounge on the sofa, or visit with Jeremiah and Lizzy. I should be ashamed. Every now and then someone gentle would see her, and want to hold the two of us, and I would let them. But it was only for a little while. They would eventually realize that a penis really did make a difference to them, after all. Or they would be getting ready to move to a bigger city where they could live freer, where there were lots of others like us.

And there were more rules. Consider yourself blessed, privileged to be here. You are being watched. Always being watched. Be polite.

Appear logical. Be plain. Don't let your disabilities show. Never cop to any mental illness.

It was hard following the rules. I was lonelier than I have ever been in my life. I had lots of small breakdowns, meltdowns, and shutdowns. I lived part time in the gray concrete of doctor's offices and hospitals, therapy clinics and inpatient facilities. Needles, tubes, splints, casts, bandages, catheters, examination tables and beds, pill bottles, thermometers, hospital gowns, and scales. I was sick so much. I had a hard time holding it together, and sometimes, I couldn't. I was spinning around all of the time.

I learned that tenure was the golden apple, and at the same time, it was the apple that Adam and Eve ate. The formula was simple for me: Say yes to the devil and forget my old lives. Forget *life*. Forget about meditation and spirituality, hot tubs, redwood trees, yoga, exercise, friendships, movies, concerts, dancing, hugging, reading for pleasure, camping, or laughing. Forget any leisurely thing. Work all of the time. There was so much to get done, and I worked so slowly, so working all the time was the only way I had even the slightest chance. When I wasn't working, I was lying awake at night, staring at the ceiling, hearing the voices of people talking when there were no people around, or walking back and forth in the house, like an animal in a cage. I did the same thing with my mind and spirit that black football players do with their bodies. I sacrificed them.

I lived in a daze, thinking that any day, I would be going back to California. I would be going back to be near my son and the rest of my families. Thinking I would be going to Pune, to live in the commune and meditate and be near my guru. I lived numb. "When am I going home?" I would sit on my bed and ask myself at night. I would bounce checks every month and try to slowly work myself out of the sinkhole. By the time I paid bills, there was nothing left, but then I still needed to eat. I stood at the counter in the grocery store, sweating, wondering if my card would be rejected. Wondering if I would be shamed again in front of other people. I was wearing decent clothes now, but I still felt like a homeless person.

The comforts that kept me going were usually random pieces of memory. I sometimes found myself back in the smoke house in the yard where I grew up, surrounded by the aromas of peppered and salted bacon, hams, loins, ribs, and beef shoulders and sides. By the scents of hickory smoke and rubbed oils and sage. Thin slats of light filtered through cracks of the boards, dissolving time, dissolving space, and dissolving my body. I could hear my breath, my heart. I would close my eyes and remember what safety felt like. I would hold on to Jeremiah and Lizzy for dear life. Sometimes, in the silver town, I would wake up from my memories on a strange lawn, with a dog barking or licking my face, or with the light starting to come to the morning and a car going by.

But in winter, snow fell, and it was quiet. And one more thing about the snow—it was a good filter. There were lots of filters in California. The hills. The fog. The ocean was one the filters. The ocean was a cure for so many things. It was a cure for darkness, because the water always held light. It was a cure for my inability to imagine the future, because it gave me a picture of what goes on forever but can't yet be seen. But along with the trees and the hills, it also gave me a mysterious filter. The ocean mist that was in the air filtered sounds so I could focus better and not be so overwhelmed. I could half dissolve in the mist and wrap around sounds rather than be buffeted by them. When the streetcar's iron wheels screeched against the iron of the track, the mist shaved off the high peaks of pitch, like an EQ dial. It softened voices and horns so that crowds became like a heartbeat. It dimmed the red of sirens. This buffer emanated from the undulating of waves, lapping at the shore in a thousand places, all day, all of the night.

But in Missouri, there was so little filtered. Everything that blew across the flat lands of Kansas and Nebraska, Iowa and Missouri, banged into my brain. There were no hills. No ocean. No fog, or mist. There were so many noises peeling away my skin. Horns and sirens. Diesel engines, grinding bulldozers and high screeching cranes. White men in loud trucks and cars threw bombs at people they didn't like, as they were crossing the street or standing on the corner. There were bombs in the revving of their engines and in the screeching of tires and burning of rubber. They were angry because the end to stretching Confederate flags across their truck windows was coming, or at least, it seemed that way in 1990. They were angry because people who weren't like them dared to be walking on the streets. Dared to be alive.

And there were so many eyes on me, as if just walking on a sidewalk made me a sideshow. It was a little like being back in the South in 1950, except there were hardly any black people. There were so many gazes lighting people on fire. I hated standing on the street corner, watching people burn. During the Vietnam War, I saw pictures of monks in orange robes who lit themselves on fire. I also saw men, women, and children being lit on fire with napalm. When I stood on the corner, in Columbia, Missouri, waiting for the light to turn, and saw people ablaze, I wondered, is this a war?

The snow was like the hills, sea, and sea mist in California. It softened noises, except, it brought so much cold.

I understood that time was against me. I understood that I needed to publish a book, but I couldn't write anymore. I had abandoned all the things that fed me. My poetry couldn't get through all the costumes and masks. I had no space in my mind, or any peace, and so poems stayed as far from me as a butterfly from a hive of bees. My first experience with the tenure clock was that I was a failure. I didn't have what it takes to make it as a poet in the academy. And so I started publishing articles and writing academic books. I cared deeply about my research projects, but I didn't *need* to do them. It was like the dreadful sensory experience of sticking my hands in mud or wet clay and weeping as a sickness spread through my body.

I found it difficult always having to explain everything, and never being able to make a statement without talking about what someone else had already said. In fact, everything about writing books was hard. I didn't always understand a lot of what I was reading when I did research, or even a lot of what I was writing, not the way others understand it. But I understood the patterns of how language worked, and the patterns of thought that went along with the words. The patterns were often more interesting to me than the thoughts. I would rather have fallen down a long flight of stairs than to have sat for hours at a computer. If I was John Henry, the computer could be my hammer. But if I was B.B. King, it couldn't be my Lucille. I had no love for it. Life wanted me to write academic books, and so they got written, because life always gets what it wants.

I learned to write good books and articles, but I never knew the people who read them. I never knew whether or not they made any difference, so I never felt like I had said anything. And being a successful scholar was about more than publishing books. One had to become "known," and for that I would have had to network, go more places and talk to more people, remember names, and stay in touch. And I couldn't do any of those things.

Getting tenure was even more complicated. I had to be what was called "a good citizen," and to somehow fit in, or at least, not stand out in the wrong ways. But it wasn't always clear what ways were wrong. I knew that I couldn't let a lot of things show. I knew that I shouldn't let people know that I was like I was, even though at that point, I wouldn't have known to use the words, autism spectrum. Looking around, everyone else seemed to communicate with each other so well, to understand how things worked. To understand what we were here for. A big part of their pleasure seemed to be the delight of having similar points of reference, similar minds. They were sometimes giddy with it.

The people in my department were perfectly nice to me, down to the last person. They were kind, supportive, and welcoming, and I could tell they wanted me to succeed. They liked me, and appreciated my thoughtfulness, and what they thought of as my wisdom. I think they also appreciated my quiet—that I was not "the angry black man" they had so much fear of.

But in the end, they would be judging me. Deciding if I could stay. To become one of them. And they were strangers, neurological typicals, and mostly, white men. I saw tides in the department turn on someone, and drown them, if they didn't fit in. It was usually a woman, burned at the stake. They put gags over the person's mouth, with their looks and their silences. They would start to look at the person the way they looked at non-academic people, the way people passing by on the streets sometimes looked at me when I was homeless, or confused, or having a day when I couldn't hold it together. I saw other people leave because they couldn't take the pressure, or because they had breakdowns and resigned, or because the sacrifice just wasn't worth it.

How could I fit in? Everyone's experiences and ways of looking at life were so different from mine. They talked about their summer homes in Colorado and vacations in Europe, and shared stories about the boarding schools they attended. There was an unmeasured distance that couldn't be crossed. If my family had lived near their families, Mama could have been "the help" watching some of them when they were children, or being paid by some of them to watch their children. She could have cooked for them, cleaned their houses, and taken them to museums and picked them up from school while their parents were working. I could have worn their hand-me-downs. I could have had a moist rag over my nose and mouth to keep from getting asthma attacks while I mowed their lawns, or while I mopped the floors of their school at night, after getting out of my school across town. Daddy could have been their janitor.

I was being asked to be loyal to a department that might ultimately abandon me. How did that make sense? And what were we, to one another? How much of what I saw could I believe in? And, what would I do if I didn't get tenure?

When I came, the university was recruiting black professors and pushing for diversity. But most of the black professors who came during those years soon left. There was no support for us. When students wrote "niggers" or other things like that in their papers, or expressed those same thoughts in class, we couldn't do anything. To support us, the university would have had to admit the problems. But it wasn't going to do that. When I talked to the department chairs about these things, they would just pause, and reflect, and say, *well, I'm sure they're really good kids.* Just the mention of the word "diversity" could set people off. It was like they had been slapped in the face, and they started defending their innocence. They started making the person who said the "D" word the bad one, like the body wanting to rid itself of a splinter.

In spring, the trees lining the cobblestone street leading from my house were pretty, in a gothic sort of way. Bending over University Avenue, a thick green arch, a tunnel. But they made it a haunted street. The songs they sang, when the wind blew, when something moved them, or when the minutes ticked by and nothing moved them at all, were heavy male whispers. They gave me headaches. They caved my shoulder blades in, so that I became the man with the crippled back.

Somedays bright golden white sunlight would come, but it couldn't rescue the brown city, it couldn't save me where I was covered by the silver light. It couldn't dissolve the dome of silver around the silver town. Sometimes pink light would spill from red buds and crepe myrtle. Day in and day out, golden beings would glow, in classrooms, offices, halls, hallways, unions, memorials, sidewalks, courts, triangles, quads, lawns, and plazas. Some of them would stay, while most would glow for seconds, with the luminosity of passing jelly fish or lanterns carried through fog. Some of their threads would reach out to mine. Some of their colors would rise out of their throats, along with the sounds, along with the pitches of words, the tones of sentences and paragraphs. Along with the echoes of laughter. Some of their colors would spread out from smiles, wrinkles, the corners of their eyes, while I listened, or watched, or mentored, or taught.

The lights and colors would change me, would change my colors. They would change my tones, my complexion, my disposition. They would hold their hands out to offer me water, but I would be so skittish, like an antelope at an African watering hole. I would drink, but never stop trembling, and so I would miss any flavor of sweetness, any sense of comfort or being refreshed. I would be hearing the whir of duties, pounding against my heart. I would be feeling the weight of noises, and the explosions of psychedelic colors from all the surrounding, crowded spaces. So I wouldn't remember that I had drank. So I would still be thirsty.

Sometimes we would stay attached, like a runner stays connected to breath, like pigment stays a part of dye, like ringing stays bonded to a bell. And eventually, the colors would help define me, like a lamp defines a shadow. They would teach me, the teacher, new meanings of things. They would be the blessings I never imagined, or asked for. And it would feel funny, then, to want to be saved from the silver town. Sometimes, then, the breath I needed to live, the quiet I needed to keep from falling apart, the distance I needed to be happy would feel like treason.

But nevertheless, I needed those things. Try as I may, I couldn't keep up. The wheel would go around and around, but each time the places would be different, would have changed. Fall semester. Thanksgiving break. Christmas break. Spring semester. Spring break. Summer session. Summer break. Each time, they would have completely new faces. New colors, new dates, new courses, new classrooms, new times, new names, new scents, new tones, new moods, new paces, new windows, new weather out the windows, new desks, new tables, new chairs, new I, and new me. I collapsed after every change. I lay awake worried, before each new season. I fell off the cliff each time a routine was chopped off like a limb, and floated for days in nothingness, like a maple tree's helicopter picked up again and again by heavy wind.

One day, snow fell. It fell like it had when I was a child. And then, the next day, it rained. It stormed. No matter where I was, inside or outside, I was freezing or getting soaked to my bones. It thundered and tree limbs broke off in the wind. And then, the next day the sun was out and white clouds drifted in the blue sky, talking to me. It was calm, and I was standing at the clothesline with Mama. The sun's heat purified me. And then, the next day, all the leaves were on fire, and every time I stepped on one, the crunching sound made me sick as a dog. And then, the next day, there were jonquils, and I could walk on the air the way Jesus walked on water. I could float like a kite. This kept happening, over and over, for the very first time. And then, the calendar said I had been in the silver town for ten years. But I couldn't remember being there that long. And then, the cycle repeated, and the calendar said, now it's been twenty years.

I was awarded tenure after six years, and then promotion to full professor a few years after that. But there was so much hollowness inside me by then that when winter came, cold winds blew through me. I experienced belonging, for moments, in my department, being respected, at times being needed. I worked hard. I made a few friends.

It dawned on me that being a professor was an ideal career. It's one of the only jobs I could have survived in. People think of professors as odd and eccentric anyway, so I haven't stood out the way I would have most other places. I've been able to spend most of my time alone. I've been around other people also obsessed, in their own ways, with organizing things. I've had summer and holiday breaks, as if we're some kind of royalty. The silver town hasn't been heaven, but it's been safe. It's been quiet. It's been like another carnival in many ways. The view out of my office window has been blue skies, the waving of green leaves on tall trees, and students streaming by at all hours. They never get older. There's laughter, and chatter, and endless promise, a window pane away.

Someday, I'll get to take off my copper mask, put it in a fire, melt it down, and make some bracelets and other jewelry. Already, I can't remember key things. Of all the papers I've written on and filled out in my life, I can't remember any of them. Applications. Grant proposals. Publisher's contracts. Tenure files. When I try to remember them, I just see blank white, and then small green hills appear in my mind, and the scent of evergreens. And then I feel happy. I look at the diplomas on my wall, so that I'll know that I really went to those schools and really graduated. As with many things, I feel like somebody else did them. Someday, the copper mask will become like all the other memories that someone else reminds me of, but I can no longer remember.

Making Lunch

There's no accounting for taste.

It's a warm September day. I'm home and there are leftovers in the fridge. I can make lunch and sit on the comfy red sofa and eat. I can listen to the quiet. I can be with the cicadas screeching their final songs. I can feel their heat almost burning me. I can try forgetting that I have a job, because when I remember my job, I forget everything else. I've lived that way for the last twenty years, but now I want to live differently. I want to remember other things. I want to remember eating. I want to remember sleeping. I want to remember my dreams. I want to remember my wife and my children. What they're doing today. Their birthdays. Their favorite songs and colors. The sounds of their laughter.

There's a small container of pasta. Some spicy sauce that Karen made with peppers and tomatoes. I love when Karen cooks. I love the way she tastes, in all her colors. I love the flambé of her smile. At night, when we lie in bed, it's like drinking moon. In the morning, it's like eating cake. I close my eyes, and the warmth of it slowly drifts over my tongue, down my throat, and into my belly.

I love when Karen makes food. In our house, I'm usually doing it. I own the kitchen, just like my mama. I try to hold things together with scents. I try to slow things down with taste. I try saying things with food that it might take me months to say if I waited for the words. I put my red apron on and disappear into the soft sizzling of green vegetables in a skillet. In slow dancing between pans and cutting boards. In the background the kids and Karen come and go. They talk, turn faucets on and off. They laugh at somebody doing something crazy on YouTube. I try organizing us. I hunt down the food. I make the fire. I try insisting we sit down at night together. They'll remember it later. And if it's never going to become a memory for me, now is all I have.

When me and Karen first met, I had just come through the portal to Missouri. I was traumatized and frightened. I was an Asperger's poster boy, determined to hold it together, to be "professional." I was the man in the copper mask, refusing to take it off. Karen was loving me, but I was just thinking about my work. Between now and then is twenty-five years. Two divorces and four children. And a moment, when nothing else was moving, and I was able to see her, and when I saw her, all my love came down, and her love and mine finally met in the middle.

But living together wasn't easy. People don't know it, but they are forests and cities of sounds. Of colors and scents. And each forest and each city has its own patterns. When I live with people, I have to find all of the patterns. I have to know where everything fits. Where the endings of cycles are. Where in the cycles I am at any given moment. What is coming next. What the moods of their footsteps are. What their paths are in each room. How long they stay in one place. If they shuffle or if they stand still. If their movements are smooth or if they are abrupt. If they are loud or gentle when they open and close the doors.

These patterns are my time, like your time is clocks, hours, and minutes. Seconds and years, and decades and months. My time is the patterns the patterns make. For a long time, finding them is all I'm doing. I'm doing it so much, I'm not myself. At least, I'm not the self other people know. I'm not the self they like being around. I'm like Victor Frankenstein. The other people in the house start wondering where I went. Who is this new person who doesn't smile, who doesn't touch, who doesn't even seem friendly?

And then, people talk, and they move things. I'll try to explain it like this. If you were living in a house with someone who was blind, what would happen if you moved the chair from where it usually sits? Or the knives and the cutting board? Or the dishes in the cabinet?

The food in the refrigerator? The keys hanging on the rack? This is not a metaphor; it's exactly like that. I see by touching the skirts of objects. I know where all of them are, all the time. I talk to them. I play with them. I listen to them whisper. That *is* life to me. It is beauty, order, sense, meaning, joy, and reason. At night, I like to walk through the house in the dark, with my eyes closed, so that I don't even see the moonlight spilling in the windows. Things come alive in the dark. They move out of their forms. The main law of objects is to never let people see you moving. But at night, in the darkness with my eyes closed, objects can move about and not violate their laws. I love to walk along the hallways and feel things reaching out to touch me. Whispering and laughing. Their touches are so soft. I love to overhear their conversations.

When someone left a cabinet open or moved dishes around, I would sometimes start crying. If a cup was touching another cup that it hated, or a smooth blue glass was up against a glass that had ridges or bumps in it, I would get depressed. The dishes were so miserable that I couldn't stand it. They would look at me as if I had betrayed them. When I stumbled over something left in the middle of the floor, or couldn't find the green pepper that was keeping peace in the crisper of the fridge, I had meltdowns.

The night I couldn't find the soy sauce was a turning point in my relationship with Karen. I was like I was as a child. I threw all of the spices from the cabinet onto the kitchen floor. I broke plates and saucers, glasses and bowls. I couldn't help myself. I felt so lost, panicked, so overcome with hopelessness.

But Karen had an epiphany that I might have Asperger's. She was trying to understand the contradictions. I could be so sensitive and warm but suddenly disappear into a cold wilderness where no one else could follow. I could be the wolf at the edge of the wilderness baring its teeth. I could be loving and connected one day and not seem to recognize her the next. I could write brilliant scholarship and poetry and yet fall apart over a missing spoon. We started going to therapy and reading more about ASD. We started talking about strategies to make living together work better. Karen found a lot of examples on the Internet of how couples like us managed. One couple lived in two houses joined by a bridge. I liked that idea, but it wasn't feasible.

So we added on a new bedroom, and the old bedroom became my study. Our new bedroom has a skylight! It lets in just the right amount of daylight. Just the right amount of moonlight. Just the right amount of stars and dark skies. The idea of adding space has saved us. I can lie in bed and look through leaves and see the blue sky and the clouds. I can open the windows and play with the wind or leave them closed and look for spaceships. I can close the door if I need to have quiet. Or I can leave the door open and enjoy being connected to my family. I have a space to work and play music in. We have our own front door that opens onto a patio where we can sit on warm days.

And right beside the patio is a piece of my heart—the flower garden I made. Working in the garden is part of my therapy. Nothing else calms or centers me more. Working in the garden is my granny's spirit. Is Mama's spirit. Is the spirits of all the generations from the plantation. The flowers in the garden have to be just right. The right bud, followed by the right stem, coming into the space at just the right speed. The blossoms have to be impeccably beautiful, quiet, and sweet. They have to be the perfect tones that hold the shadows and the light together but apart in waves that spread out like stars. Have you seen the way the lines between shadows and light move like dancers? They have to be the perfect dancers doing the perfect dances. The colors you can't paint. The tones we can't capture. This garden is a palace I'm building for the spirits. Jeremiah and Lizzy, Esau and Beulah can have a sanctuary, over there, between the pink rose blossoms, the wild purple sage and hibiscus. Granny is on the yellow blossoms of bell flowers, with the Buddha. Between the yellow blossoms of coreopsis, other spirits of my ancestors come and go. Grandma Betty. Octavia Butler. Grandma Addie. Daddy. Han Shan. Frida Kahlo.

Me and Karen also worked on other things. We monitor my social energy like a diabetic monitoring blood sugar. We talk about little things before they can happen. Like when we're going out. I used to have tearful meltdowns in restaurants if the food wasn't just right on the plate. Or if there wasn't enough sauce. Or if the sauce touched the rice. Or if the colors of the food weren't arranged correctly. Or if the heat inside the food wasn't at just the right temperature. It was like the world was ending. I felt so hurt. I felt like I had been watching the sunset and someone had suddenly yanked the plank from under my feet and I had fallen into cold water and was drowning. I've learned to contain myself when things are not perfect. At least some things, most of the time. It helps when Karen pats me on the arm. It also helps if we go to mostly the same restaurants. Ones where the owners know me. The waiters are familiar. They are generous, patient. The chefs put special memories in the food. Special warmth that stays, like smooth stones heated all day by the hot sun.

I work on things at home too. Like, before I go into another room, I try to remember to be mindful. I try to remember that the room I'm going into is probably going to be too bright. I try to remember that there is probably going to be a dirty dish in the sink. I try to remember that there are going to be broken patterns in the cabinet and refrigerator. I try to remember my family's feelings. I try to remember that they are more important than the patterns. That I can take time later and repair the patterns that are broken. I try to remember that it's easier to fix the patterns than it is to repair the bruised feelings a meltdown could cause.

Me and Karen have worked on moving things around, to avoid problems. Like the blue glasses that I love so much. That talk to me when I am blue. They are no longer in the kitchen cabinet. They're happy in a closet in my study, where their dignity can be preserved. I open the closet doors, and stand there, and listen to them speak with the voices of spirits from the plantation. With the voices of blue bottles in my granny and mama's kitchens. In the whispers of broken blue glass in the rubble of slave cabins and of fallen and burned houses back through the woods where I grew up. I stand there and me and Ruby turn to moons, turn to skies, turn to rivers. We turn to wood in vanished houses. We turn to spirits in the garden.

There's things in many secret places around the house. Pretty boxes, baskets, and tins filled with spirits from different times in my life. So many pretty things! So many sweet-smelling things! Seashells, pieces of wood with faces in them. Rocks, feathers, and matchboxes. Ribbons, hair, and baby teeth. Tarot cards, postcards, and greeting cards. Bones, notes, and small bottles of scents. Coins, and oils, and essences. Pretty colored paper. Crayons and watercolors. A paintbrush and torn-out pictures from a magazine. My granny's old thimble.

A nutmeg. Leaves and dried flower blossoms. Rose and mango soaps. Musk and jasmine lotion. Threads, and hair, and twine. Bits of broken glass and plastic and metal. When no one is home, I open a box. I open a basket. I open a tin and shower myself with spirits.

By and by, I learned everyone's patterns. I became familiar with everybody's sounds. By and by, they learned my quirks. Karen sees me. Her love sings around me like poetry. Her love sings around me like morning birds, singing through the mist. I don't have to hide the Aspie. The repeaters can come out. They can repeat until the body is released and the ghosts are free. Ruby can moan aloud. I can treat her to soft fabrics that make her skin radiant. She can lounge on a soft bed in the suburbs and not have to worry. I can speak in tongues, as long as it's not too late at night and Karen is trying to sleep. I can never know what day it is or what city I'm in. And it's all right.

Let me tell you about our wedding. It was full of magic. It was going to be outside, but it rained for days. It wouldn't stop raining. Streams a foot deep flooded across our yard, rushed past the house, and emptied into the already flooded streets. So we had the wedding in a church. But it was too late to book a place for the reception. So we needed someone with a magic wand, and Karen had one. We put a big tent over the driveway. We cleaned out the garage and decorated it with sheets and lanterns and balloons. Together, with the tent, we had a reception hall, with sit-down tables with white tablecloths. With music and bouquets of flowers. Our families and friends came. People cried when before their eyes we became clouds on the altar and floated out of the church. But we don't just float together. We walk on the ground. We take walks. Karen helps to keep me grounded. She reminds me of things that need attention on earth but understands that I am often in my spaceship.

I can understand better now how hard it is for neurotypicals to understand Aspies. I know now that the difference is more profound than most neurotypicals can imagine, but I don't really know how to explain it. I'm no Temple Grandin. I've become more aware of how many private rituals and how many must-be-this-ways I need just to function from one minute to the next. Everything, every day, all day long, is a part of a perfect system that no one else can see. Like long rows of dominoes standing on end, the first one falling into the next, and so on and so on. If one of the dominoes doesn't fall, if there's too large a space in between and one of them doesn't tip the next one, my hold on things disintegrates. I tiptoe or skip from lily pad to lily pad in a deep lake. Trying to explain my systems is hard. I've never had to. I don't know how to. I've never thought about them as anything separate from life. In fact, I've never really thought about them. It's like thinking about breathing.

There's a two-days-old half of chicken sandwich on the bottom shelf. There are leftover potpies from the dinner I made last night. There are greens and falafel and lasagna from earlier in the week, and fried apples and biscuits from breakfast. But which food will fit best with the red of the sofa, the saffron of the throw pillow, the jazzy blue of the painting, the deep green of the soft velvet easy chair? Which food will pick up the sea of afternoon light, shimmering with déjà vus and intermittent waves of feeling? What flavors and colors on my plate will turn the waves into a picture of a place—the thing you call memory? What combinations of scent will help me stay grounded longer than a second?

I know what you're thinking. Why don't I just eat whatever I feel like eating? The reason is because I never just feel like eating anything. I'm not sure what that would be like. Every food choice is tied to something else. The pasta sauce is Karen's love. And so I don't really want it to get eaten. I want to put it in the small refrigerator in the study and enjoy it endlessly, to preserve it. It's how I eat a pastry. I take a bite and then wrap it and put it in a special place on a cabinet shelf. And I think about it and smile the rest of the day. The next day, I make myself wait, and then, maybe in the afternoon, I take another bite. Almost giddy, I close my eyes and savor it. I do that until it is gone.

The food is the thing and the memory of it at the same time. Because I can't remember, once I eat it, the experience is gone. So I keep holding on and, all too often, the food spoils. The greatest pleasure is not from the food but from what it captures and how perfectly it does it. My favorite meals are leftovers from three or four good days put together. Four really good days of recipes that carry the flavors of four days of special closeness with my family. I eat feelings, moods, memories, and pictures in my imagination.

But today, twenty minutes have passed, and I'm still standing at the counter and looking at the options. I even try making rules. Rule number 22 is, Eat what is oldest first. So I rearrange the containers on the counter in the order of their age. But that doesn't work.

Rule number 28: Set aside dinner for tonight and then eat whatever is left. But then I start thinking about which kids will be home and which ones won't, and what time, and who will have already eaten. Once I start thinking about the kids, I start forgetting about lunch.

When I am with my children, I feel so satisfied and content. I feel as if I have managed to do something good on earth. In the spaces of the children, there is such goodness. Even when they are noisy sometimes, their presences are like quiet music. They struggle with the meanings of many things and I struggle to keep up with their growth. It happens so fast. Before I can process wherever they are, they are somewhere else. *The Velveteen Rabbit* and *Goodnight Moon* blurs with *The Hunger Games*. I have been a good dad in part because so much of me is a child. I loved reading to them. Playing games and going to the park. I already miss things from every stage of their lives. How could they be so grown up? When did they suddenly turn into such people of their own? Why don't I feel that any time has passed?

My first son, Nick, is all grown up now, working as an attorney in New York City. He's a man. He decided when he was ten years old that he wanted to be a lawyer, and he never wavered. He was born in a yellow house, in the Mission District, in San Francisco. We had five friends there who were midwives, and a doctor who was a friend and sannyasin. We named him Nicholas Nesta Seth Folly. Nicholas means "victory of the people." Nesta is after Bob Marley. Seth was one of the angels channeled by Claire Prophet. Nick is so kind, so passionate about truth and justice. When I think of him, or talk to him, I see all the years of his life. I feel all the moments. I feel such pride and joy. One day he was standing beside a redwood, in a redwood forest, and the tree lit up. He comes to visit several times a year and goes with us to visit my mama and family in Virginia in the summer. But sometimes I wish I could just walk over or drive over or take the train over and knock on his door, talk for a bit over tea, and hug him.

My second son, Kahlil, was born in a hospital in Columbia, and I was also at his birth. I am thankful every day that I get to spend all of his growing up with him. He is at my house half the week and at his mom's the other half, but we talk and text every day. His mother, LuAnne, lives five minutes away, and we work in the same department at the university. I met her at a folklore conference in Louisiana, shortly after being released from a mental inpatient facility. After being in the facility, I realized that I couldn't wait for the spaceship to come and get me. That I couldn't wait until I could go to India and live in the commune. That I couldn't wait for the hypothetical day when I could get back to California and walk by the Pacific, and hug a eucalyptus or a redwood, or throw myself on the ground in a green meadow. That I had to find a community here and now in order to survive.

So I took down the note card I had on the closet mirror. It read, *Don't ever get married again. Remember, you can't live with people. It doesn't work!* And I started making a list of qualities I thought the perfect wife would have, and a list of prospective people to marry. I started looking for that wife. But as soon as I met LuAnne, my son started appearing to me in dreams. After that, I knew we were supposed to be together, and so I threw my list away. What I didn't know was that we weren't supposed to stay together.

After she completed her MA at UCLA, she decided to move to Missouri, and for a year we lived in my yellow house. After a year, we moved to a nicer split-level house in a neighborhood that felt like the suburbs. It was quiet, with a huge backyard edged by woods and a huge front yard where we planted flower gardens. We had Kahlil, and like with my other relationships, things fell apart. The difference this time was that, after the divorce, we worked on things so that we could be good coparents, and even at times, friends.

We named our son Kahlil Ravi Roth-Folly. We named him after Kahlil Gibran, the mystic and poet who wrote *The Prophet*, and then Ravi, which means the sun, brightness, warmth, giver of life. It turns out that he is the mystic, the philosopher. He likes to ponder the nature of the universe. What is time? What is the nature of the spirit, of consciousness? He opens his magic box and music comes out. He sees the patterns in colored dots and graphs on the computer screen and makes them into songs. "Beats," they call them. He paints beautiful pictures with beats, the way I used to write poems or study insects. Sounds that are not music hurt him. A whisper sounds like a shout to him. The hum of other people's sorrow weighs him down and breaks his heart. There is a joy, there is an innocent goodness that emanates from him like from a field of purple hyacinth. There is a bubbling lightness from his face, as if, like me, he came from the stars.

Also, like me, my son Eze comes from another planet, but a different one than I did. He stands at the window, or outside, gazing up into trees and clouds, levitating. He feeds his geckos religiously and knows the birdcalls of every North American bird. He is the gentle scientist. I saw him in a premonition before he was born, and

I called Karen in San Francisco to tell her about him. "King" is what his name means, and he gives a new meaning to it. He is the king of kindness. Sometimes his teenage anxiety is like water in a dam that is overflowing but cannot break. Then I want to hug him, but he hates touch, textures, almost as much as someone with autism spectrum disorder.

My daughter, Asa, is a strong wind. In Igbo, her birth father's language, her name means "beautiful." If beauty is a whole thing, it's the perfect name for her. She sees people, and sometimes I think she sees spirits, but she won't look at them. She's afraid.

She might become a therapist someday, and if she does, she'll diagnose patients with a glance. She'll go straight to the marrow. Her insight sometimes gets ahead of her, the way a teenage boy's body gets ahead of him, when his legs are suddenly longer. Every year, she bursts out of a new cocoon. She's now you see her, and now you don't. Even the chrysalis is always in motion. In the motions of words, of smiles and laughter, and at the center, a heart fragile as a poppy. Sometimes she goes by on her magic carpet, and I smile at the coco butter, tangerine, papaya, henna wind left drifting on the breeze.

But now for lunch.

Rule number 42: When all else fails, eat soup, and then go to the window. Take a few minutes. Let my eyes stop focusing so that I can see. Melt into the greens and the blues. The clouds. Look for the glimmers of spaceships.

Prahlad received his MA and PhD in folklore studies and sociolinguistics at UC Berkeley and UCLA. He currently teaches folklore, film, creative writing, and disability studies in the English Department at the University of Missouri, Columbia, where he has been a professor since 1990 and where he has been the recipient of numerous major teaching awards.

Prahlad has published two books of poems, *Hear My Story and Other Poems*, and *As Good As Mango*. His poems and creative nonfiction have appeared in literary journals such as *Fifth Wednesday*, *Water~Stone Review*, *Copper Nickel*, *Pleiades*, *The Chariton Review*, and *Natural Bridge*.

Prahlad has also published critical articles and books on black folklore including *Reggae Wisdom: Proverbs in Jamaican Music*, and *African American Proverbs in Context*. He has edited the three volume set, *The Greenwood Encyclopedia of African American Folklore*, and the one volume *The Greenwood Student Encyclopedia of African American Folklore*.

In addition to his creative writing and scholarship, Prahlad is also a songwriter and musician, who plays multiple instruments, including the African mbira. He released his first CD, *Hover Near*, in 2008, and is now working on a second CD.